Easy Steps to Becoming a 5 Witch

Easy Steps to Becoming a Witch

Gilly Sergiev

Thorsons

Thorsons
An Imprint of HarperCollins*Publishers*
77–85 Fulham Palace Road,
Hammersmith, London W6 8JB

The Thorsons website address is: www.thorsons.com

Published by Thorsons 2000

10 9 8 7 6 5 4 3 2 1

A catalogue record for this book
is available from the British Library

ISBN 0 00 710221 6

Printed and bound in Great Britain by
Martins The Printers Limited, Berwick upon Tweed

Dedication

Emil – my love

Jean – my friend

and to all you Witches on the journey

Empowerment!

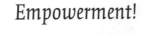

Contents

Introduction

> This is Magic; that which is a blessing and a gift from
> the Feminine Principal, more ancient than time,
> within and without the Universes.
> Exposed to those who would use it wisely.

Book of Souls – Akashic Records

At my birth in this life I had the 'official markings' of a Witch, which in the old days would have almost certainly caused me to be drowned or burnt at the stake! Luckily, times have moved on from then and in this new Spiritual Age anyone can be a Witch! As long as you want to believe and your intentions are honourable, the Goddess will welcome you.

In the old days Witches

were reviled and treated horrifically, when in essence a true Witch is a servant of nature and the whole purpose of Witchcraft is to serve, to heal and to help. This book is an attempt to interest and inform people of the beauty and mysticality of Witchcraft and the true essence of serving the forces and spirits of nature, so that if we all try together, we can make a difference and pull ourselves back from the man-made destructiveness of our future and make our world a clean, safe and loving place to be again.

My life has been more than enriched with this knowledge and I am certain yours could be too. It definitely is a positive issue if you have some of the markings, because it probably means you are on a return visit to this plane from being a Witch in a previous life. Because so many Witches, Healers, and people ahead of their time, were drowned or burnt in the old ages it released a lot of mystical and good energy into the ethereal cosmos. In order to bring this energy back to the physical world, these spirits were born again in a new age where they could continue to develop their talents for the good of others. This probably explains why now of all times – with the increasing number of mature spirits being reborn – people are beginning to take more and more of an interest in mystical things; society

as a whole has relaxed its attitude because it recognizes the good that mystics do.

With my help you too can become a Witch in five easy stages. Witchcraft is a natural science that can aid and strengthen people and do good for our planet. As the new Millennium has begun and we are finally in the Age of Aquarius, now more than ever, we are feeling a kind of 'cosmic pull' towards mystical and ethereal life-styles. We are finally beginning to think deeply about ecology and economy, about saving our planet and our souls, before the greed and despair of recent years engulfs us. Now is the time we all need to pull together to save our precious world and try and reverse the negativity that we have allowed to fester.

Witchcraft (white Witches practising green magic) is all about helping people and energy, it is about kindness and goodness and spirituality, it is about healing and love, it is about nature. Anyone thinking they can put a hex on their worst enemy is reading the wrong book!

Remember: what goes around comes around and if you practise hatred or Black Magic the balance of harmony in nature will make sure it is returned to you a thousandfold!

Anyone can become a Witch. If you have the strength of mind and determination – and most importantly **want** to become a Witch – you are half-way there. Once you have faith in the Goddess she will answer you.

Strangely enough not all Witches like to jump about in the moonlight wearing nothing but a bright smile and chanting spells! Most Witches I know have everyday jobs and appear pretty much like everyone else except, perhaps, if you look again you may see signs of an individual peeping out! Most people these days seem to know of a friend or colleague who is slightly odder than the majority or who is always the one to 'have a go' at things, no matter how idiotic, perhaps wear clothes that don't fit with any formula of the day – anything for a laugh! These are the people, like Witches themselves, who have the courage to know who they are as individuals and be who they are, regardless of any horrified or petty discrimination against them. I should imagine you are one of these brave individuals!

It is possible that for some time now you have been wanting to explore a part of yourself that manifests itself at office parties or in the pub on Friday nights! Every so

12

often, there is a part of you that feels different, reckless, apart from the norm and you know that inside you is someone very special wishing to appear. Perhaps you have been interested in mystical things for some time. Perhaps you have had contact with aliens or invisible friends. Perhaps you feel that you are in touch with a different plane than the one most people go around on. Whatever it is that sets you apart, do not despair! Help is at hand!

There are so many people who are special and different in their own unique way and it is very important that we all recognize our individual talents and unique abilities and commune with the spirit of life around us which flows through everything. It is especially important RIGHT NOW because we have entered a new Millennium and this is a very special and potent time in the great Calendar of Being in our Spiritual Age. The Age of Aquarius that we have been talking about for so long is finally with us (having started in the last month of 1999) and with the change from the Age of Pisces to Aquarius this is a time for new beginnings, new environments, new horizons and beliefs and power of the individual. So you've taken a step in the right direction by starting with this book, now chill out and read all about it and discover the **5 Easy Steps to Becoming a Witch!**

Step 1

> The Witches stood black as the Night and Dark and Cold it was outside...

Book of Souls – Akashic Records

⭑ GOD AND GODDESS, ELEMENTALS AND YOUR GUARDIAN ANGEL

The basic beliefs of a Witch are very personal to each individual. Witchcraft is not a religious creed or dogma which you learn and are cowed by. It is a belief in love, harmony, balance and truth connected to the planet and the spiritual essence of nature. There are the basic frameworks to work within but whether you work in a Coven or as a Singular, you must trust your own reactions, beliefs, subconscious.

The main points are always:

✳ Do Not Deliberately Harm Others;
✳ What Goes Around Comes Around;
✳ Keep Love.

Within each framework of beliefs is the basic idea of **God and Goddess** being the Creators. They exist both separately and as part of each other. God is attuned to the masculine and is known as Cernunnos, Father, Yang, the Spirit of the Sun, Osiris, the Horned One, The Lord, etc., and the Goddess, attuned to the feminine is variously known as Cerridwen, Mother, Yin, the Spirit of the Moon, Isis, The Crone, The Lady, etc. It is up to you what you feel most comfortable calling the Lord and Lady and if you are unsure of how to address them, don't worry about it, start by calling them Lord and Lady; in time the right names will come. Hecate is one of the

15

names of the Goddess of Witches and one that I feel comfortable calling her.

The story behind the God and Goddess is a cycle of renewal and rebirth. The year is composed of a variety of celebrations which together create what I call *The Great Calendar of Being*. The main eight important festivals are called Sabbats and they celebrate the story of the God and Goddess:

* **Yule Sabbat:** A celebration on 21st December when the Goddess gives birth to the God and all rejoice and celebrate.

New Moon – Maiden

Full Moon – Mother

Dark Moon – Crone

* **Imbolg Sabbat:** A celebration on 2nd February when the Goddess recovers from the birth and all rejoice and celebrate recovery, the renewing of life and the beginning of the Earth's awakening into Spring.

* **Ostara Sabbat:** The Spring Equinox and a celebration on 21st March when both the God and Goddess travel together to celebrate fertility and reproduction in the Earth and animals around them.

* **Beltane Sabbat:** Occurs on 1st May when the God and

The Great Calendar of Being.

The Sabbats

Vervain

Foxglove

2nd February — IMBOLC — Goddess recovers from birth of God. Rejuvenation	**21st March — OSTARA —** God and Goddess walk the land. Reproduction
1st May — BELTANE — God and Goddess unite. Fertility	**21st June — LITHA —** God and Goddess celebrate Healing
1st August — LAMMAS — God impregnates Goddess. Conception	**21st September — MABON —** God leaves & Goddess rests. Thanksgiving
31st October — SAMHAIN — Goddess mourns for God Death	**21st December — YULE —** Goddess gives birth to God Re-birth

17

Goddess unite and encourage fertility and healing. Food sacrifices are made to them and bonfires burnt.

* **Litha Sabbat:** On 21st/22nd June. Another fire festival incorporating bonfires when the God and Goddess are both at the height of power and we celebrate the power of love and health.

* **Lammas Sabbat** (also known as Lughnasadh): Follows on 31st July/1st August. A harvest festival when the Goddess becomes pregnant and we celebrate the bringing in of crops.

* **Mabon Sabbat:** The Autumn Equinox on 21st September when the Goddess is resting and it is a time for thanksgiving and silent vigil.

* **Samhain Sabbat:** Celebrated on 31st October (which is also recognized as Halloween) which is when the God has departed and the Goddess is alone. We use this time to communicate with spirits of the dead, either our friends or others that wish us to learn from them. At this time, the doors to the otherworld (sometimes called Summerland) are wide open and humans and spirits can mix freely.

Then the Sabbats continue again with the Yule Sabbat when the God is reborn. The whole idea is closely linked to the harmony of nature and the cycle of life, death and rebirth.

Although the Creator is made up of the God and Goddess, the dominant entity is the Goddess, from whom the God is born, dies and is then reborn. Some people find the idea of worshipping a horned God rather worrying as it seems to imply the Devil, but this is far from an accurate representation; Witches do not believe in the concept of the Devil. It is important that one understands fully that the Horned God is absolutely nothing to do with the Devil of the Christian religion (which was a later addition by the Church). The Horned God is the God of physical and symbolic animal fertility, of strength and nature,

signified by his horns. Remember that this is an ancient God and was around long before the invention of the Christian Devil.

Unfortunately, because the frightening nature of the Christian interpretation of the Devil was drawn from the ancient image, the original Horned God was then thought to be a variation of the same thing. Over time, the original ancient God of nature became confused with the vile interpretation called the Devil. Thus, in the medieval days a lot of nonsense was attributed to Witches about worshipping the Devil, which was far from the truth, but which caused a great many innocent deaths.

The idea of a central Mother Goddess has been around since time began, from various ancients as far as Egypt and Cyprus to the Druids of our land. The very first religion in Egypt tells of the sacred isle of Benben – which rose from the lake of Nu and spat forth the Gods – possibly included a Mother Earth Goddess figure. Around the time of 2134 BC shallow graves were found in Egypt containing baked clay figures of a wide-hipped female figure with arms extended to the sky, generally agreed to be a Mother Goddess and possibly known as The Great White Cow. She may also allude to the Goddess Hathor, who conceived and gave birth to the God, died and was reborn. (Spell 554 *The Pyramid Texts*.)

There are many similarities between these early times and the later explanations in the Bible of Mary and Jesus; for example, the Mother of God, Mary, gave birth to Jesus, who then died and was reincarnated. Keep an open mind.

The God and Goddess have their own special names by which you will refer to them. These names are personal to you and the more you get used to spellworking and communion, the more you will find your own special ways to address them and be addressed by them. There are a lot of different thoughts discussed on how and where you obtain your own Witch's name (which is a name you decide to call yourself as a Witch) and although it ultimately comes to you from the Goddess, it is a name that you decide on and use in your day-to-day Witch's life.

However, there is another name that some Witches have, called the **Secret** or **Sacred Name**, which is specifically requested from the Goddess and, if given to you, is accepted that you will never repeat it, but hold within your mind as your personal gift from the Goddess. In many ancient religions, again such as the Egyptians', worshippers believed that if anyone knew of your secret name, they had power over you and this was one of the reasons

you kept the name to yourself. Mothers would give their children two names but would never divulge the secret name so that if anyone wanted to put a spell on their child by using their name, it wouldn't work, because the name that the child was known by was not the secret, true name.

It is similar in Witchcraft. You only use this secret name when spellworking or communicating with the spirits by yourself. When I asked the Goddess for my secret name I fell asleep thinking of all sorts of nice and ancient names and while I slept I had a visit from the Goddess who told me a name that took me completely by surprise as it was not a name I would have ever thought of! However, the more I thought on the name and practised saying it in my head, the more I realized that although it was extremely unusual, I actually liked it! What's more as it was a name unlike anything I would have thought of, it was proof positive that I had not chosen it myself but was given it from the Goddess. Strangely enough, a week after being given my secret name I walked into our local library and immediately saw a book in front of me with that strange and ancient name on it – the book was about the life of this person and to me it was a powerful acknowledgement from the Goddess. I hug this name to myself and it gives me a potent link with the Goddess, knowing that she named me thus.

The Elementals are the spirits of the Elements, namely:

✳ Fire – (attributed to the South and masculine);
✳ Water – (attributed to the West and feminine);
✳ Earth – (attributed to the North and feminine);
✳ Air – (attributed to the East and masculine).

They are spirit entities that control their own element and are used very much in spellworking and prayer. They can help you enormously and must always be treated with respect, it is no good conjuring up Fierce Storms just because someone has annoyed you! Each one of us has parts of the elements within us; we are mainly composed of water (Water), we breath air (Air), we have a temperature (Fire), and eventually our bodies return to and become part of dust (Earth). As we are eternally linked to the elements – rather like a family – when we call on them to help or to accentuate spellworking, believe me, they will show themselves!

Inside the **Special Place** or **Temple** wherein you do your magical workings and communicate with the God, Goddess and the Elements, will

also remain your **Guardian Angel**, otherwise known as Protector or Spirit Guide. This is the good spirit that guides you and protects you. Again, in time, you will learn to know the given name of your Guardian Angel. Depending on your particular talents, you will probably be able to communicate with your Protector and even see your Protector. However, even if it takes you a while to develop these talents be aware that the guide is there, watching over you and protecting you.

Always commune with your guide in a loving way. Remember their power is all-encompassing and you are merely requesting their

protection and
support, not
demanding it! If they
communicate with you
that is a blessing and
should be treated with
reverence. Always
thank your guide and
ask for their blessings
and close each working
with a special ritualistic
prayer, cleansing the
atmosphere, your
special place and tools.
Be aware that your
Guardian Angel is
always there, watching
over you and helping
you with your good

intentions. Whenever you are concerned or worried, communicate your feelings in prayer or verse – whatever comes naturally to you – and your guide will assure you and protect you. Some people have Spirit Animals that work as their angels, it is not something that you choose, but rather something that you become more and more aware of as you do your workings.

It is generally believed that the Bible is a collection of stories written by man to explain the basics of Christian Religion. In fact, when the Bible was first written, it had large sections devoted to reincarnation. However, the men that put the Bible together deliberately left out the passages about reincarnation because, for some reason, they did not want it known. (Possibly as a way of keeping power over the people, because, if you know for certain that you will be reborn, you are not going to be afraid of dying, and unfortunately, one of the prime weapons of power is fear.) However, it is interesting to note that they could not remove the most powerful image of reincarnation, namely that of Jesus rising from his tomb!

Pagan religion flourished long before the Bible was written and it is believed that some of the festivals, such as Christmas, were actually chosen dates of earlier

Pagan festivals.

The point is that most religions have very similar concepts. If you look at Egyptian beliefs, it was of the Creator, Atum the Supreme Being (i.e. the God), who sneezed out Shu (male – similar to Adam) and spat out Tefnut (female – similar to Eve), from whence all the other deities (similar to the disciples and Saints) came. Before Atum, there was a void, nothing (similar to the beginning of the Bible when God created the world).

The Hawaiians believed in 12 tribes who lived in the Sahara and then when the water dried up, one tribe moved to Hawaii and the other 11 moved to Egypt, where they built the great pyramids using Kahuna Magic before dispersing. (Similar to the 12 Tribes of Israel, the 12 disciples, etc.) Many ancient religions, such as the Incas and the Mayans tell of a terrible flood (Noah's flood in the Bible) which has now apparently been actually confirmed and dated to between around 10,500 BC and 6,500 BC.

I believe this was the time when the waters finally closed over Atlantis, thereby sinking the Islands. I also believe that very soon the ruins of Atlantis will be found again with modern technology, which will confirm a lot of argued-about theories. An excellent book for reviewing this is *The Mayan*

Prophecies by Adrian G. Gilbert and Maurice M. Cotterell.

If you can keep an open mind, you are more likely to discover the truth than by closing your mind and refusing to look. Scientists and sceptics alike, although they do marvellous work, are still only interested if something can be literally proven. Even when marvellous evidence is put forward they can still close their minds to the realities because it isn't scientific or can't be literally proven. People who have that way of thinking may be able to do wonderful experiments,

but will they ever really know the truth?

The reason there are so many mystics, is because they are in tune with something so marvellous and they want to spread the word and help others. In *The Mayan Prophecies* there is a lead that suggests the Mayans may have discovered how to unleash the powerful properties of the right side of the brain (the artistic side, dealing with seeing into the future and spatial construction) by wearing magnets on the hypothalamus area of the head, the third eye of the head and over the left ear of the head –

thereby connecting the left hemisphere (logical) with the right hemisphere (artistic). Does this sound like mysticism or science? I've used scientific terms to describe a mystic possibility. Who knows, perhaps mystics are in fact people who have already learned how to access parts of the brain that most people don't use. Keep an open mind and learn. After all, how can you prove the voice of the Goddess when she communicates with us each privately and secretly?

I hold the personal belief that we are on a journey in this life to find our true essence, our soul, ourselves. Although this life seems a trial of obstacles and difficulties, we have all been given secret and special powers with which to help us. By using these abilities within us we find out who we are and then when we have found that which we are, our bodies die and we (our essence) moves on to the next spiritual plane where we acquire new attributes, such as helping others through the spirit world. If we don't find our purpose in this life, we have the chance to be reborn, reincarnated, to try again. Very simply put I believe that this is our purpose in this life and in the whole scheme of things.

 *Step 2*

❛...They were to be killed
Accused of things they hadn't done
and I was one...❜

Book of Souls – Akashic Records

☆ APPEARANCE

It is vitally important for each Witch to have his or her own individual appearance which is special to them. You need to 'tune in' to your creative persona which will lead you in the right direction. For example, think about these things:

✳ Which year between, say, 1799 to 1999 interests you the most?

✳ What was the fashion like for that period?

✳ What were the colours and shapes predominant in that time?

✳ Do you relate to those too?

✳ What are your favourite colours?

Not every Witch likes to run around in a crumpled pointy hat and black cloak you know! (Although there is nothing wrong with that if it feels right for you!) Find your style. A lot of Witches I know prefer to wear natural fabrics because this keeps them in tune with the natural forces around them. Some Witches are happier in pale, light colours while others feel more at home in fiery, loud colours.

Your personal style and taste is somewhat determined by your astrological sign. There are 12 basic personalities which match the 12 signs of the zodiac. Obviously, from those 12 basics come many hundreds of thousands of variations but all these are in keeping with the 12 modes.

From a general overview of your sign you can obtain a more in-depth understanding of your personality through techniques such as palmistry, scrying and reading the heavens at your particular time and place of birth. For example, I am an Aquarian with nearly all the planets in the sign of Aquarius when I was born. Without knowing why, I have constantly been drawn to Air and Water symbolism throughout my life: my colours are blue, white, silver and green; I adore swimming, rain and all connections with water; I have travelled extensively; my mind is constantly situated in the clouds and I am attracted to a sense of space. To balance this, illnesses I have had in the past have been connected with breathing and circulation and when I was very young, almost drowning! There is more of course, but if you yourself, look into your personality and the appearance you are most drawn to, I am sure that you will find a link with your astrological sign and the astronomy at your time of birth!

Whatever style you choose, stick to it and keep it, particularly when you are in your 'Witch mode'. You may not be able to go to work dressed in 'Witch mode', it may make others feel uncomfortable or perhaps your neighbours would object. For whatever reason, if you simply can't wear your Witch gear at all times, then keep it separately wrapped in tissue in a special box, or on a particular shelf. This sacred space will in time take on its own magical aura.

If your particular strengths are healing ones, you may find you automatically lean towards colours such as green, blue or yellow and favour gems such as amethyst, jade or amber. If your strengths are more tuned to communication you may find you are predisposed towards navy, black and silver with attraction to gems such as aquamarine, blue sapphire, and azurite. If your strengths are more in the area of worship and psychic ability your colours should be white, purple and gold and your gems will probably be pearls, moonstone and opals. If your strengths favour relationships your colours are probably pink, red and purple with gems such as ruby, beryl and diamond.

These are just suggestions of relevant gems and colours to particular skills and the more you research into these areas the more likely you are to be surprised at how your automatic choice favours your particular skills and personality!

There are many marks which used to be linked with Witches – a sixth finger, webbed toes, extra birth marks were all indications. Do not despair if you do not have any particular marks, in this day and age transfer tattoos are a marvellous alternative! Do you yearn for a particular hair colour? It could be a calling from your previous life. If it is a strong feeling then go with it, after all, there are marvellous products around these days. A white streak in otherwise dark hair is often favoured and can easily be achieved with hair

dye! A lot of witches use their own favourite colours in their hair as streaked areas, and if you do not want or cannot go permanent, then find hair pieces attached to grips or bands which can be put on (and taken off) at a moment's notice! Although my own hair is a naturally dark colour I have always known since very young that it should have been light! As soon as I was sixteen I had it bleached and have been varying degrees of blonde ever since! It feels right and by listening to my inner voice I have found my outer face!

There are wonderful glitter products in the shops for hair use, as well as body and face use, and I would definitely recommend a few of those! Witches look extremely good in glitter and the constant shine and energy given off by the glitter will enhance your own aura and psychic abilities. Flowers and leaves, whether real or false, twined in hair look gorgeous and subconsciously convey to others your natural beauty and connection to the Earth.

Nails are important to Witches, as they create an illusion of long, slender hands and allow the ritual pointing and hand waving an extra power. The energy from the Witch shoots down the arm, through the hands and then, like an arrow, is narrowed through the nail as a shaft of pure power. If you can't grow your nails, how about false nails, stick-on or semi-permanent? They are all easy to obtain. You can pierce your nails with various tiny rings and symbols as well as paint them with magic inscriptions which will all aid your mystic power.

How do you feel about shoes? Do you like the pointy toe or clumpy platform? Accessories are very important and there are marvellous ones about these days. Charity shops are a very useful source of Witches stock because they have so much of everyone else's clutter that the mixture usually means you can find anything if you look hard enough! How do you feel about scarves? They are very inspiring when long and floaty and mixed together in your particular colour scheme. Charity shops are particularly useful when looking for individual pieces of jewellery, chunky beads, etc., and most Witches can never have enough of those! Look for crescent-shaped objects, attuned to the Moon, or cat-shaped, attuned to a familiar, or broom-shaped attuned to cleansing. If you buy your gear from charity shops not only will it be as individual as you, but you will be immediately helping others too, which makes a very good start!

With any item bought second-hand, it is always a good idea to do a ritual cleansing first. The item will have ingested the spirituality and personality of the person who owned it before and you must cleanse the item so that you can ingest your own spirituality and personality into it. To cleanse the item you can either steep it in salt water, then leave it to absorb the sun's rays for at least an hour, then pass it through clear, running water, finally patting dry and leaving it on your altar; or if the object cannot be exposed to water for some reason, pass it 3 times through the smoke of a burning incense stick on your altar, 3 times over the stone, 3 times over the chalice of water and 3 times through the smoke of the candle flame.

Witches, because their very

nature is attuned to the elements, will most likely favour natural fabrics, such as wool, cotton, linen and silk. However, fabrics such as velvet and the variations on velvet such as velour, have a very sensual feel and appeal to the instincts of a mystic because the sense of touch is stimulated. As we have progressed in the world of fabrics it is now possible to get marvellous imitations of fur and leather as well as exotic fabrics such as rubber and paper. It is totally your choice. What feels right, what you are pulled towards, are the fabrics for you. It takes a lot of courage to stick to your beliefs but it is immensely satisfying when you have finally found your style.

Because, once you have found your style, you will immediately feel better and more able to concentrate on the job in hand; you will have related to your inner self and listened to your needs and therefore be confident in yourself.

The more you wear your Witches gear, the more comfortable you will feel and eventually it should merge with your everyday life in a satisfying way. Do not be surprised if you find yourself being copied, look on it as a compliment and understand that that particular individual is perhaps just starting to take the steps towards finding themselves too. When you are a Witch you can afford to be deeply understanding because you are just that little bit extra special!

Do not despair if you don't fit into the ideal size 12 figure! Size has nothing to do with looking good or having style. Believe me, I should know! Larger sizes simply convey more love and a generosity of spirit, so it is not unusual that a lot of Witches have problems with weight. The reason for this is that Witches try to contain their weight and size into a minimalist proportion to please and fit in with society, and yet at their very essence lies giving and generosity which means that their natural size should be large! It can sometimes become a constant struggle throughout life trying to balance the two opposites and my advice to any Witches with weight problems is that as long as there is no medical danger with your size, just relax and be who you are. You are beautiful.

There are many clothes shops now that include or specialize in larger sizes and a very well-known chain in most high streets that seems to concentrate on floaty, glittering, unusual colours and fabrics – one would think made exclusively for Witches!

If you are really concerned about your particular shape or size, there are ways to get around this. Beauty spells and diminishing spells work temporarily, but you have to keep doing them with the phases of the waning moon. This is difficult to do regularly, but is essential before going out to an exciting party!

From a practical point of view black is always a good colour for Witches. Wearing layers of clothes is a clever way to 'cut' the outline and fool the eye. If you are large, straight skirts are more flattering than A-line. If you buy clothes that are one size larger than you need, you will look as though you are losing weight and it is more flattering to have material 'flowing' as opposed to 'hugging' the body! Keep socks and tights the same colour as your skirt or trousers, so that the 'line' is not interrupted, this gives a 'leaner' look to the figure.

The best advice for a super figure, whatever size it may be, is to invest in decent underwear! A well-structured bra or lycra knickers for example, will do a great deal for your shape even before you've added your clothing! Depending on your hair or skin colour, go for neutral colours, such as gold, silver, brown, black and grey. Keep the whole outfit attuned to one particular colour and then add a 'splash' of something really stunning such as pink, red, violet, diamanté or aqua in the form of a scarf, necklace, loose belt, gloves or hat, or undershirt or bra, and you will look fabulous – because you are fabulous!

mistletoe
mistletoe
mistletoe
mistletoe
mistletoe

Step 3

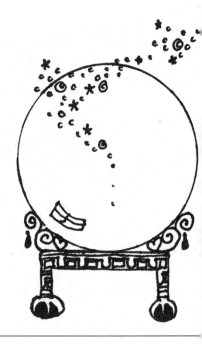

> *... A cry rent the air*
> *a scream, a laugh*
> *Not evil, but sad...*

Book of Souls – Akashic Records

☆ TOOLS

Every Witch has a plethora of tools! You don't need many to start off with and will probably increase your stock as you get more familiar with your needs. However, here are the basics.

A **crystal ball** is used for Scrying. This is an extremely

Crystal Ball and Mirror

useful tool for looking into the future or past and you can tell other things too. It gives you information about people and places. As you become more in tune with it you can learn information about people and places. Best of all it looks really pretty!

A crystal ball can be any size and is preferably made of quartz crystal (although glass or other crystals can be used). Quartz crystal is the most popular and in ancient times was thought to be frozen ice! From a scientific point of view quartz crystal is full of electrons and magnetic energy which abound within the structure, and when compressed hard enough can produce electricity. As a result, with regular use, one can commune with the energies and connect with the electromagnetic current inside the crystal to produce stunning effects such as healing and potency to spellworkings and Scrying.

Crystal balls are not easy to come by and everyone must find the one that calls to them. Antique yards, second-hand shops, some chains of jewellery shops, or car-boot sales are all very good places to look.

Wherever you look, if you are determined to find one you will do. Try a spell to call to your crystal ball – it will hear you and guide you to it.

When you have found your crystal ball you need to personalize it. Firstly, wash it in a solution of vinegar and water mixed together and then polish with a clean, soft cloth. On a new or preferably full moon, sit with it outside so the rays of the moon can be soaked up into the crystal ball. Whenever possible, sit with your crystal ball in the moonlight because this will empower it. However, do not let the sun's rays touch it as they are detrimental to its energy.

Sit with it in both your

hands or supported within a magic circle and gaze into its depth for a good 10 minutes every day. Let your mind drift and your eyes relax, but stare hard into the heart of the crystal ball. Different people get different results but the primary objective is to encourage a misty swirling of cloud within the ball. This is the signal that time is going backwards or forwards and from this you should then perceive images and pictures, similar to Scrying in fire or clouds, although a lot clearer! In time, you should start to communicate with it in a very advanced way. It takes practice for successful Scrying and the most important trick is to remember to relax, then things should come easily to you.

Always when not in use, wrap it in a dark cloth or bag and store it in the same place. It is very important to keep your crystal ball out of the light as this can interfere with the images that come forward, so when reading, keep the lights dimmed in your room and if possible, use candlelight.

The Witch's **mirror** is similar to the crystal ball and again used for Scrying. In the very ancient days, Witches used dark polished stones such as black onyx and obsidian. In Turkey examples of finely polished discs of obsidian have been found which date back to

Neolithic times. To this day scientists are unsure of how the process of polishing the stones to such a high intensity was achieved. But to my mind these stones are definite evidence of early Scrying mirrors! From ancient times to today practically any polished or mirrored surface has been used for Scrying. Liquid has always been a popular

HENUT TAWI

medium using such objects as bowls of water or natural and ancient pools.

The mirror you use is again your choice, however the most popular and easiest mirror to start with is usually silver-backed and painted black. You should really take the glass out and paint the back of the glass black and then return it to its setting with the unpainted side out, this then gives the painted side a depth. You might like to personalize it around the edges with mystical words or pictures, but this is not a necessity.

As you did with the crystal ball, you need to take your mirror out into the moonlight in order to 'energize it'. After that you can use it anywhere you need to. A dimly lit room is recommended to avoid distractions.

You should look into the mirror to see images, in a similar way to the crystal ball. Although the mirror is not mainly for the future or the past as in the case of the crystal ball, you can also communicate with good spirits through the mirror and conjure up results and answers to questions. Remember always that you are in control of what you see.

You should keep your mirror in a dark place, such as a black velvet bag, and always replace it after use. Clean your mirror after use with a clean dry cloth and say your ritual prayer of thanks.

Cauldron

A **cauldron** is basically a large cooking pot! It is used for preparing magic potions and spells and is a very special piece of equipment to the Witch. A cauldron – like all other tools – is individual to each Witch. It does not have to be a large black three-legged bowl with a hook for the fire, which seems to be the most popular myth surrounding it! It is a bowl-shaped cooking utensil that is just as happy on a gas oven! You will find the cauldron that is special for you. Obviously it has to be fire proof and the better quality pot that you buy the more potent your spells will become.

You can use the cauldron to grind things (although a pestle and mortar is recommended for this really), mix things, stew things, steep things or boil things depending on your spells or magic recipes. It is not recommended to use your cauldron for every day cooking as this will confuse the mystical energy and at best your pot will not work and at worst the spell residues may overflow into your Sunday lunch!

Keep your cauldron in its own space and use it only for conducting your magic spells and potions. After use, always clean it thoroughly and wipe a small amount of oil, such as walnut oil or almond oil, around the inside. This will keep the pot steady in its applications and protect it from any outside influences or changes, so that your spells will always be fresh.

Magic Wand and Broom

The **magic wand** is a stick-shaped object which can be used in incantations, spells, even stirring your cauldron. It is useful for tying different coloured ribbons, string or cord on, if you are doing ribbon, string or cord magic! It stirs up the Ether and brings potency to your spells.

A magic wand made of hazel is very popular, also ash or willow. But it could just as well be a black plastic joke shop stick if it means something to you and your character. You may find a stick lying in the road or a stick shape that appeals on a shopping trip, and once you have got the initial wand piece, you can then decorate and enhance your wand with your own chosen special items. Crystals and stones tied or stuck to the wand are good, ribbons tied around the wand, feathers, beads and special objects all have a place on the wand. The fact that the objects are special to you is the main consideration because by absorbing your potent energy, your wand will respond to your wishes.

Once you have chosen your magic wand, you need to give it a name. Place your wand on the altar in your special place or temple and sit in front of it staring into your mirror. Incant aloud 'Goddess of the Moon, this Wand I show, bring forth its name, for me only to know, so let it be.' After concentrating hard you can sometimes see swirls of cloudy lights and then words or letters pertaining to the magical name of your wand, alternatively, these words may form in your mind. Using your innate knowledge use these letters or words to form the name. If possible inscribe the name on your stick in small writing, but do not reveal the name of your magic wand to anyone. (You might like to cover over the name with material or paint so that it can't be seen.)

After naming your magic wand clean it by rubbing a cotton wool ball with oil of frankincense over it for spiritual fruitfulness. When using your magic wand in spellworkings, always refer to it by its name. After use, keep your wand inside your special place or temple at all times in order to concentrate its magic forces. If at any time your magic wand becomes disturbed in any way (by being outside the temple area, or being used by someone else) re-clean it with frankincense and leave on your altar for one day and one night. If by any chance someone finds out the name of your magic wand it will become useless and then you will have to dispose of it, ritually, and try and obtain another one.

Should you treat your magic wand carelessly you will find it harder to obtain another working one and the name may not come forward, in which case you may find it harder to be able to use one

successfully in the future. A good witch always has respect for her tools.

The **broom** is used in ritual sweeping out or cleansing of areas – specifically your special place or temple. If you need to do magic elsewhere, your broom should always be used first to clear the area of negative energy. The broom should ideally be made of hazel or willow twigs tied to a central wooden pole with natural strands (such as hemp). The central pole should be weekly polished and fed with oil of oak or lavender.

The broom is used at the beginning and ending of all ceremonies or spells. It can also be used for sleep flying when you are meditating or in certain spellworking. You may even use it to visit others! By envisaging another that you would like to visit the broom offers you the opportunity to 'connect' to that person both physically and mentally.

Herbs, Salt, Oils, Candles, Incense, String, Ribbon and Cord, Magical Stone

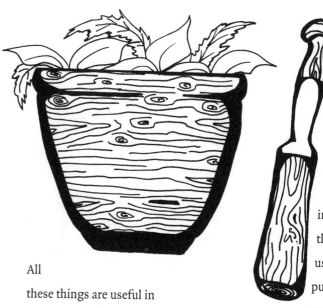

incense which is also used for clearing the room of previous spells in order to refresh and restart.

Salt is kept in a special dish on the altar for ritual use, it represents purity and value and protects one from

All these things are useful in conducting spells. **Herbs** are used in their different forms as ingredients in spells; different **oils** are used to attract different attributes to the spells; **candles** attract forces – again depending on their colours; as does

harmful entities. The magic circle is often composed of salt for these very reasons.

Candles are important and depend on their different colours in order to use their various properties. These are the most common colours and their main properties:

* White – purification
* Gold – finances
* Silver – divination and scrying
* Blue – travel and movement
* Green – health
* Pink or red – love
* Purple – senses and spirituality
* Yellow – happiness

String or ribbons are used tied to your fingers, around spells or to your magic wand. They are tied in various ways when you are doing string, cord or ribbon spells. Ribbons have different meanings for the different colours and are attuned to different parts of your body depending on your incantations. The most potent area of your body for ribbon, cord or string spells is your third eye. This is the area exactly in the middle between your two seeing eyes and about one centimetre upwards. This is your mystical eye which sees far more than any other.

The ribbon, cord or string is placed on each area of the body that you are attuned to for the working of the spell. For example, the heart, for matters of love; the legs, for matters of travel; your mouth, for communication; and so on. Ribbon, cord and string are also used to symbolically bind people and spells in ritual magic working to stop negativity.

The **magical stone** is used in various spells as a symbol for the Earth and should always be kept on your altar in your special place or temple. The magical stone gathers energy the longer you practise your magic and should not be removed from the altar of your temple at any time. It is the centre of your home and all your workings are centred indirectly around it. It may be used for laying offerings such as flowers, herbs, spells, etc. on it, it may have string, cord or ribbons tied around it to directionalize its energy field. It can be touched by the Witch in her incantations, but whatever used for, it must always stay in the same place and only touched by the Witch. The magical stone is a separate object to the stone used for the symbolic elemental Earth which sits with the other Elementals: Fire, Water and Air.

Special Place or Temple of Worship and Shrine

Your **special place** or **temple of worship** is the area that you choose in which to carry out your magical workings. A real marble or stone temple with columns and statues at the bottom of the garden would be ideal, but unfortunately most of us cannot run to that extravagance! It does not matter; if you are interested in having the area in the garden you can create a bower from wooden or plastic frames and cover it with sweet smelling vines and flowers, such as honeysuckle, climbing roses and ivy.

If you would prefer to have it inside your house you could choose a spare bedroom. Hang the room with silks from a sari shop or material from a second-hand shop – whatever feels right for you.

First of all choose your special place or temple and decide that this is where you will do all your workings and then consecrate it. The important thing to keep in mind is that this is the dwelling of your spirit guide, the God and Goddess and the Elemental spirits, so you would do well to create some picture or statue in reference to these.

You will need an altar on which to place your workings and which – if you use your imagination – can be made of almost anything. A small table, two boxes with a plank of wood over, a box on its own, a wicker basket, a window ledge, etc.

Over your altar should be placed a white cloth – it is up to you whether you wish to decorate it with pictures or names. On top of the altar should be two candles (usually white unless you are conducting a spell which has the use of different coloured candles); a gold candle, which stands for the Fire Elemental; and incense which stands for the Air Elemental. In front of the incense should be your chalice of water which stands for the Water Elemental and a special stone which stands for the Earth Elemental.

If your altar is big enough it can be useful to keep your crystal ball or mirror on, a special dish of salt and also your Book of Spells. However, try not to cover your altar completely as you will need space for the mystical energies to flow harmoniously around everything. Above the middle of the altar against the wall, or if that is not possible near to the altar, it is nice to have a picture or statue of your Spirit Guide, God, Goddess or all three.

To the right-hand side of your altar should stand your particular chair and no-one else should sit in it. Choose and decorate it to your particular leanings, which could be opulent and vibrant in colours and materials such as gilt and velvets, or plain and simple such as a beautiful piece of carved wood. It could be the ultimate 1960s plastic designer chair or antique leather –

anything which is special to you.

Your chair is where you sit when you are meditating, concentrating and conducting and if you think about it, the more you use the chair for magical workings, the more imbued with magic it will become and therefore will take on its own personality linked with yours. The only time it may be necessary for someone else to sit in your chair is if an extreme form of healing is needed and you particularly want your magical energy to be ingested by the sitter. If this is the case then when the healing is over you must ritually cleanse your chair and sit in it whenever possible to restore the magical energy.

Amulet/Talisman/ Holy Relic

Amulets are charms for protection and **talismans** are charms for a purpose. These are powerful objects, special to you that you should carry about you and use in spells when you need a very strong boost or a personal angle to your magic. They take on your energy the longer you have them about you and are very potent.

They can be any object that has some special meaning to you,

although it is best to look in the realms of mystery and good fortune, in order to give your amulet or talisman a good start. For example, simple ideas include a four-leaf clover, crystals, piece of the Berlin Wall, a small statue, unusual money pieces, a vial of holy water, finger nails wrapped in cotton wool, unusual shaped stones, or a chicken's wishbone sprayed with gold. A very well-known amulet is the Holey Stone (also known as a Hag Stone) which is a stone with a natural occurring hole in its centre. These are often found on the beach where the sea has worn away a hole. The hole is supposed to be the place where negativity gets trapped. Interestingly, some ancient foreign coins were made with holes in the centre which served the same purpose.

The best way to carry a talisman or amulet is around your neck. It is easy to find a leather thong with a pouch of some sort attached, into which you place your talisman. If you carry it around your neck you are less likely to leave it in the pockets of your other jacket! Be careful when swimming, bathing or showering though, as natural fabrics and fibres eventually rot when regularly exposed to water! If, for some reason, you have to leave your amulet or talisman at home, find it a special box and spend the most you can afford on this box, as it is a very special object indeed and should be kept in the most luxurious of surroundings which ennobles its special status. Remember that a luxurious surrounding does not have to cost a lot of money! A scrap of velvet, a gold pen, fine silk, diamanté beads, etc. can all be found in charity shops or jumble sales, but when glued together in various shapes and patterns, can transform even the humblest of matchboxes!

In order to make and consecrate a talisman for someone else, you need to know details about the person the talisman is being made for. These include their name, date of birth, the day on which day they were born, their favourite colour, and the details of why the talisman is needed. You also need to have items which relate to and concern the person in question, such as a clip of their hair or nail as well as coloured paper, ribbon, pen, oil, herbs and at least one object concerning their wish such as a photograph. You then combine the above elements into a personalized charm, writing on the paper,

enclosing a photo, the clippings, etc, and finally bind it all up in some relevant coloured paper (green for health, gold for money etc.), tied with coloured ribbon.

Place your talisman on the altar, light a gold candle for the Sun and a silver candle for the Moon. Place your chalice with water to one side and special stone or Earth opposite. Place an incense stick in the centre. Call on the God and Goddess to bless and empower your talisman, using your own words, ask the spirits of the Air, Water, Fire and Earth to bless and empower your talisman, again using your own words. Sprinkle a few drops of water on the talisman, wave the incense over the talisman, let a few drops of candle wax fall onto it and sprinkle some small pieces of earth over it. Finally rub the special stone over it – whilst praying for blessings.

Sit quietly and think about the use of the talisman and the good it will bring for the person it is for and use the relevant spell pertaining to that person. For example, the *Wish Upon A Star* spell is useful for people that seem to continually have bad luck and need

improvement in their lives.

When you are ready, draw a healing and cleansing circle around your altar or table and complete your ritual. Yourself, or the person it is for, should carry the talisman next to the body whenever possible. If its purpose is long-term then it should be placed in an area relevant to your long-term use, for example if you are a cook, in your kitchen; if you are an artist, in your studio; if it is to aid sleep or dream of the future, under the pillow; and if your preference is for entertainment, in your most entertaining room!

The Great Calendar of Being – Feast Days and Sabbats

These are some of the important celebrations in a Witch's **Great Calendar of Being**, which include the **Sabbats.** I have shown the similarities to present day feast days and celebrations as well.

Candlemas – 1st January (New Year)

Twelfth Night – Twelfth day after Yule – 2nd January

Imbolg Sabbat – 2nd February

Feast of St Valentine – 14th February

Feast of St David – 1st March

Feast of St Patrick – 17th March

Ostara Sabbat – 21st March – (which is also celebrated as Spring Equinox – 20th March – Day and Night are equal in March)

Mothering Sunday – a celebration of all women – 2nd April

Feast of St George – 23rd April

Beltane Sabbat – 1st May – (May Day)

Litha Sabbat – 21st June – Summer Solstice – (Sun stands in middle of June, also known as Midsummer – Longest day)

Lammas Sabbat – 1st August – Start of Harvest

Mabon Sabbat – 21st September (which is also celebrated as Autumn Equinox – 22nd September – Day and Night are equal in September)

Feast of St Michael – Michaelmas – 29th September

Samhain Sabbat – 31st October – End of Summer, Festival of Dead (Halloween)

Celtic New Year – Beginning of November

Feast of St Andrew – 30th November

Yule Sabbat – 21st December – Midwinter Solstice – (Sun stands in middle of December)

Familiar, Pentacle and Nudity

These are three very common subjects associated with Witchcraft that invoke feelings of worry or even terror in most people. I would like to reassure you that it is nonsense to feel worried about these things and I shall now explain why!

A **Familiar** (or Wizard's Famulus) in the old days used to be thought of as an animal (most often a black cat) that talked to the Witch and suckled on the Witch's extra breast! This is rather a revolting idea and certainly not correct, it should be thrown aside with Witch hunting, hanging, burning and dunking, but I will explain how it came about.

Sometimes people are born with extra (unformed) breasts, similar to multiple nipples on animals such as cats or dogs. They can have one or more – up to six, tiny breast markings running from beneath their own breasts down the body. They are, in reality, a form of birth mark and a lot of people have them removed by surgery. Men can have them as well as women. This unusual marking usually runs in the family and is a genetic inheritance.

However, in the past, these markings were seen as signs of the Devil and a sure indication that you were a Witch with the proof of the extra breast for the Familiar to feed from. Yuk!

The reason many Witch's have cats as their Familiar is simply because cats have a deep sensitivity to their surroundings and can tune into the spirits that are all around. How often has your cat suddenly stared at a seemingly blank space and 'frozen'? They do it all the time because they are extremely sensitive animals.

Your pet doesn't have to be a cat and can be any animal you have an affinity with. Your pet will communicate with you but not

through actual words! Pets tend to communicate in
sound-noises as opposed to actual word-noises.
However, the more you listen to your pet the more you
will identify each particular
sound, rather like learning a
foreign language! If you are in
tune with your animal you can sense
and read their thoughts and wishes. They
can warn you of problems and cheer you
up and generally be of help around
your magical life. A Familiar is not
essential to your workings but as
well as being sensitive (and

therefore a kind of tuning fork) to ethereal influences they can also be a great
help and comfort.

If you mention the word **Pentacle** to most people they will probably
hiss at you something like 'ooh the sign of the devil!' No it is not! A Pentacle
is simply a five-sided star figure. Penta means five – that is all. Whether
people use this very pretty symbol to conjure up the Devil is up to them – but

3

that is **not** the meaning of Pentacle and certainly not something a Witch would be interested in doing.

A Pentacle is an ancient and beautiful symbol of a five-pointed star, examples of which have been found in tombs of Egypt. It is a magical symbol which represents protection and is very useful when creating an altar or table for your magic uses. The points of the star can represent the four angels, Michael, Gabriel, Auriel and Raphael or if you prefer, the disciples, Matthew, Mark, Luke and John and the fifth point represents the Spirit of the Moon; the God and Goddess joined together; Isis and Osiris; Jesus and Mary; Thoth and Hathor; Cernunnos and Cerridwen; Creator and Spirit; Lord and Lady; whatever your name for the God and Goddess is.

You can decorate your Pentacle with holy

words, names, symbols and colours, whatever is special to you, and as you pray over your Pentacle the magic energy and purity will increase. It is a very beautiful shape to concentrate on when spellworking or meditating and the more you put into your Pentacle in the way of prayer and worship and thanks, the stronger its magic power will become. Whenever you stand inside a Pentacle you are totally protected from outside and unhappy influences.

Finally, **nudity**! I will write this in a nutshell because it is not a necessity and totally up to you whether you decide to go skyclad! However, in short, it is NICE TO BE NUDE! We came into this world naked and we go out of this world naked and in our most natural state we are naked. Our hang ups about our naked self are all self-taught. It feels lovely to be outside amongst nature unhampered by clothes and with the sun's rays warming your body or the cloud's rain bathing you – try it and see!

The reason Witches take off their clothes when doing rituals is to get nearer to their original selves and closer to nature; so they can feel the elements around them and on their bodies. It is very difficult to feel the breath of the life force of air on your skin if you are wearing cord trousers and a woolly jumper! Obviously Witches don't walk around naked all the time and there are different clothes for different times. It would be quite thoughtless to walk down Oxford Street in the nude as sadly one would probably be arrested! This is why Witches use the countryside and the privacy of magic places. They are not trying to draw attention to themselves, they are simply trying to commune with the natural essence of life in their natural state.

If you don't feel you are ready to be seen in your natural skin or are too self-conscious, Witches can wear fabulous robes that represent themselves in rituals, with beautiful colours and fabrics. You don't have to take your clothes off – but it does feel more natural and that is the whole essence of what you are doing – being natural with nature.

Book of Spells and Book of Dreams

Your **Book of Spells** (also referred to as a Book of Shadows), like all your equipment, is extremely special to you. The book is an open book that grows daily as you add your newly discovered spells to it. There are basic well-known spells around, as old as time, and you can start your book with these.

It is good to start with spells that have been published by Witches already, but in time you will add to your book the spells you have discovered for yourself and which you have found work with your talents. Decorate your book with magic words, numbers and symbols that are particular to your personality and don't hesitate to write down within your book anything magical that occurs to you. You can refer to your book as it gets larger as, no matter how clever you are, in time you will not remember all the spells that you accumulate!

Keep your Book of Spells wrapped in a piece of cotton and if possible on the altar of your special place or temple. Do not let anyone else read your Book of Spells. These are your potent tools to use for the good of others and the environment and certainly not something to trivialize.

Foretelling events by dreaming is known as oneiromancy. Your **Book of Dreams** is kept by your bed and at any time that you have been dreaming you must wake yourself up and immediately write it down in your book. This is a lot harder than it sounds and takes

some time to perfect because if you wake from a dream at 3.30 am it requires a lot of willpower to stay awake, find a pen and start to scribble! However, even if your writing is a scrawl, or it is the middle of the night and you can't see what you are writing, persevere. It may be that you only get parts of the dreams, but once you start writing, anything that you can remember, you will find other parts of the dream start appearing too. This all takes practice of course, but it will grow. In time you will get into the habit and begin to read your dreams and act on their messages. You may find yourself automatically waking up at a particular time each night with the dream fresh in your conscious thought and eventually you will even begin to shake off the desire to go straight back to sleep!

Dreams will send you omens, tell you the future, good luck or bad luck and advise you of each coming event. If necessary, consult a dictionary of dreams, there are many about, but remember to include all aspects of your dream no matter how tiny so that you get a correct reading. As in all things, this will take time to perfect, but the more you practice the better you will become. Your Dream Book will grow like your Book of Spells and be a valuable tool.

Magic Circle

A **magic circle** is a large circle usually drawn on the floor with the Pentacle inside it wherein you do your magic. It can also be envisaged as a circle of white light in the air and its purpose is to protect and strengthen your magical energy. It is not necessary to have a magic circle but it can lend a strength to your spells and workings as well as protect your workings and helping you to concentrate.

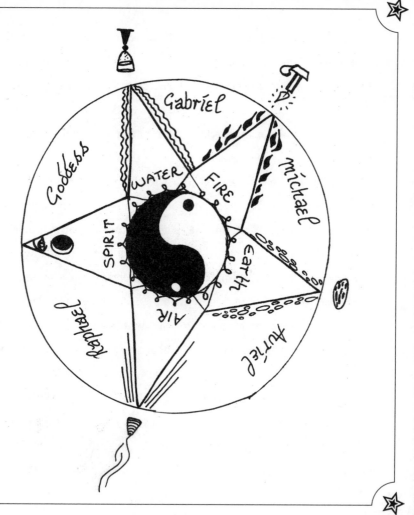

Some people find they are more attuned to magic circles than others. If you prefer, use a circular table and decorate that. Each Witch makes his or her own magic circle and – as in all things – is particular to him or her. But however you choose to personalize your circle the main idea is the same. First, find the area that you want to dedicate to your magic workings. This can be in your house, your garden, in the countryside… Wherever this place is, it is purely used for your magic and so should be private to you. Obviously it is your choice whether you invite people or clients in, but ultimately, it is the sacred place where all your magical energy convenes, your temple of worship.

Draw a large circle in a substance such as chalk, or use flour or salt on the floor or carpet. If you are outside and cannot use these items then make a large circle with natural objects such as straw, stones or sticks. Alternatively make a circle of white candles. You may then like to draw an inner circle within the large circle to create a border.

Within that border you can then write your magic names and between each name draw a Pentacle (the 5-pointed star). Some of the popular names used in Egyptian times are Atum, Amun, Hathor Anubis and Isis, but you may prefer names of angels, for example

Michael, Gabriel, Auriel and Raphael; or the names of the disciples, Matthew, Mark, Luke and John; or names in a different language or ones that are particularly special to your talents, for example Thoth, patron of writers; Ptah, patron of craftsmen; Imhotep, patron of physicians; Hathor, patron of love and so forth.

Use the centre of the magic circle to stand or sit in. Place in it your table, altar or pentacle and do your spellworking. The purpose of the magic circle is to concentrate the magical energies and protect your workings. Whenever you enter or leave the magic circle, cut a doorway with your Witch's knife through which you can come and go. A doorway will emphasize the sense of your circle being a sacred place and will seal the protective forces inside it. Remember at the end of your workings to always seal the doorway closed before closing the magic circle.

Chalice

and

Witch's

Knife

Athame

~ Chalice ~

~ Chalice ~

~ Chalice ~

The **chalice** is essentially a special goblet used for drinking water and wine or doing ritual spellworking and sprinkling the blessed liquid. The most famous chalice of all was the Holy Grail and chalices are widely used in Christian worship for sharing in the blood of Christ in Communion services.

The design of the chalice is your choice. My own chalice was found in a jumble sale and is carved from polished wood with inlays of ebony. As soon as I saw it I knew its purpose and it really called to me. I didn't buy it at first, which is unlike me as I normally act on instinct, but half way around the room, I suddenly felt worried and realized I was concerned that the goblet would be sold. I hurried back to the stall where my chalice was waiting and quickly bought it. The sense of relief I felt as soon as it was in my hands was enough proof to me that I had the right object.

The Witch's knife, also known as an **Athame**, is used only for ritually cutting ingredients for spells, such as herbs, flowers, ribbons. The knife should always have a black handle on which you can inscribe something personal to you if you desire. It should be small in size, similar to a small dagger, kitchen knife or even penknife. The blade should not be sharp as it is more concerned with the ritual of

cutting ingredients rather than actual cutting –
and nobody wants accidents! The blade is
placed in the chalice of water,
dipped in the dish of salt, passed
over the fire of the candle and
smoke of the incense and laid on
the sacred stone when ritual
spellbinding. The blunt blade of
the knife should be wiped with
oil of oak for posterity and placed
in front of a pink or
green crystal to
strengthen its use
and energize it
with either love or
healing when not in
use.

The Lords of the Watchtowers

The Lords of the Watchtowers are the four elements that protect you when working within a magic circle. There are many ways to summon them but the general ritual of invoking them is done once the magic circle has been drawn around you.

Using a compass if you have one, place four white candles at the four points of the compass: north, south, east and west. Light the candles. You then take your athame or magic wand and point it firstly to the candle in the east and say, *'Welcome, Lords of the Watchtowers of the East, Lords of the Air, I invoke ye to witness this rite and guard the circle.'* You then point to the candle at the south and say, *'Welcome Lords of the*

Watchtowers of the South, Lords of the Fire, I invoke ye to witness this rite and guard the circle.' Now point to the candle in the west and say, *'Welcome Lords of the Watchtowers of the West, Lords of the Water, I invoke ye to witness this rite and guard the circle.'* Finally point to the candle in the north and say, *'Welcome Lords of the Watchtowers of the North, Lords of the Earth, I invoke ye to witness this rite and guard the circle.'*

Having completed this ritual you are now safely within your magic circle and also guarded and witnessed by the Lords of the Watchtowers. You can now proceed with your spellworking, celebrations, rituals, whatever you wish...

Once the workings are finished you then release the Lords from their guardian positions and thank them. Once again, point your athame or magic wand to each candle in turn and say, *'Lords of the Watchtowers of the East, Lords of the Air, thank ye and with good dispatch, joyful dispatch, I close the circle'*; then *'Lords of the Watchtowers of the South, Lords of the Fire, thank ye and with good dispatch, joyful dispatch, I close the circle'*; *'Lords of the Watchtowers of the West, Lords of the Waters, thank ye and with good dispatch, joyful dispatch, I close the circle'*; and lastly *'Lords of the Watchtowers of the North, Lords of the Earth, thank ye and with good dispatch, joyful dispatch, I close the circle.'*

Agrimony

Step 4

❝...Touching me slowly
drawing me nearer
deeper and deeper
aaaaaaaaAgh...! ❞

Book of Souls – Akashic Records

✩ SPELLS AND SPECIAL RECIPES

Spells are as individual as you are. As you become more used to your role and more comfortable with your spells you will find they become more potent and trip off your tongue. Although there are increasing numbers of books around with Witch's spells, ultimately, you should learn how to develop your own. The Goddess or your spirit guide will help you to discover your own magic, while your increasing general awareness of herbs, moon times, oils and so on will inform you.

It is important to develop your own magic because these spells will be the most powerful spells for you. However, there are some important rules with spells that you should be aware of:

1 Spells should only be used for the good of others. If you are tempted to wreak havoc or harm on another for no reason, it will do you no good, as all hatred spells reverse back to their originator, so all that will happen is your life will get more miserable. However, if you have just cause to spellwork negativity on someone due to their deliberate wickedness to you, or in the name of justice by calling on *Maat*, the Egyptian goddess of justice, there are ways to protect yourself and ensure that the wrong-doer gets their deserved retribution. **This kind of spellworking is only used in extreme cases.**

Remember when casting spells:

* circling or encompassing the spell with fire **ignites** the spell with life;
* wafting and passing the spell through incense **breathes** life into the spell;
* sprinkling or dowsing the spell with water **feeds** life into the spell;
* and burying in earth **grounds** the spell into life.

2 These are all ways to bring alive the spell but it is helpful to know which spell is attuned to which element. For example *Hor-Pa-Khered* was a healing god in Egypt and it was believed that by pouring water over his image while reciting a spell in his name, the water became imbued with magic powers to cure illnesses. But if, for example, you wanted the water to become imbued with love energy, then an image of *Hathor* or *Isis* would be used.

3 If you know the true name of a deity or lifeform you can call on that image to bring alive your spell in their name.

In ancient Egypt the names of various snakes and scorpions were known and used with barley bread, garlic and salt as common healing spells against snakebite; 'scorpion herb' mixed with wine or beer was used as a common healing spell for scorpion stings. The individual names of snakes who harmed were many, but three were known as *Mehen*, *Hereret* and *Apophis* and by calling their name aloud the Egyptians believed they dominated the snake and could make the snake work for them (as opposed to against them), and thereby nullify the deadly bite or sting.

Meretseger the protective serpent goddess, *Selket* the protective

scorpion goddess, *Wadjit* the protective cobra goddess and *Nekhbet* the vulture goddess were commonly placed around the home for protection. Once you knew the name of your god or goddess, you had control over it. That is why one of the greatest gods of Egypt, *Amun*, was also known as 'The Hidden One', and had amongst many, a name that no one knew of. Unfortunately, by trickery, *Hathor* in her fighting image found out his secret name and was then able to conquer him. This point is worth remembering when you finally find your secret name (given by the Goddess and which you should divulge to absolutely no-one! see page 21)

 You can make signs with your hands in order to ward off evil:

* **The Horns** – index and little finger extended, the rest of the fingers tucked into the fist. This sign will simply send back any negativity to the ill-wisher.
* **The Cross** – similarly, crossing the fingers when sending back negativity mentally, will protect you from any rebound.
* **The Pyramid** – a pyramid shape made with the two thumbs and two index fingers, joined together and placed at centre breast or third eye, will ground your protective aura when in a negative

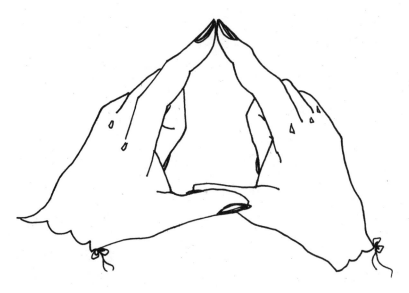

situation. You can also use the Pyramid to view with your third eye when scrying or looking into the future. This takes some practice but is worth trying. With your physical eyes closed, you place the Pyramid in front of your third eye and concentrate hard on the images that come into your mind.

* **The Blessing** – the first two fingers extended which gives power to your spellworking.

* **The Deer** – the first finger and

thumb are curved to form a circle and the final three fingers are extended, creating the horns of the Deer. When incanting or making a talisman move the hand symbol over the talisman or incense in a circular movement, three times.

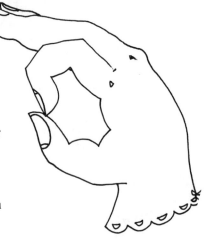

There are many hand symbols which add power or deflect power as one wishes and these can be collected and stored in your personal book of spells. You may find that some signals feel particularly comfortable and work more effectively than others. These will be where your special strengths lie.

The Moon

The Moon waxes (increases) and wanes (decreases) its appearance each month. It starts with the New Moon which is quite difficult to see but gets brighter as it continues its journey in space. Halfway through the journey the moon is completely bright; it then starts to enter the waning period and loses its brightness until it is completely dark, then it starts all over again with the New Moon. The cycle is: New Moon, Waxing period, First Quarter (when the Moon has travelled exactly one quarter of its quest around the Earth), Waxing period, Full Moon, Waning period, Last Quarter (when the Moon is travelling in the last quarter of its quest around the Earth), Waning period, back to the New Moon.

The Moon is directly linked with the Goddess, she is the Spirit of the Moon and when spellworking it is useful to know the position of the Moon – whether waxing or waning – because this directly affects your spells.

New Moon: To comprehend or realize something

Waxing Moon: To attract or add something

Full Moon: To increase and enlarge something

Waning Moon: To reduce or remove something

For example, if you are doing a spell to get rid of something such as warts, negativity or an unwanted boyfriend, then it is best to do that during the waning of the Moon; as the Moon wanes, so will the problem. If you are doing a spell for increase, such as job prospects, health or fertility, then obviously do it during the waxing period of the Moon which will increase your chances of success.

The Moon has a tremendous power and gravitational pull which controls the tides of the water on Earth (the Sun and the Earth are involved too) but its influence over our bodies is often overlooked. As the majority of our body is made up of water the Moon directly influences our elemental selves, which is why some people are more prone to release their originality during particular phases of the Moon. An old Aunt of mine was said to go mad every Full Moon and dance naked in her house, but that wasn't the case at all, she was merely in-tune with the Moon and worshipping in her own way. Of course, to the outsider it probably did look somewhat disturbing, but luckily we have moved on a long way since those times! Another ancient Aunt used to carry me as a very small child to an upstairs window and sing goodnight to the Moon before going to bed. We would look out of the window together and see the Moon and sing 'Goodnight Mistress Moon, come again and we'll see you soon, we'll wake up and call out, Goodnight Mistress Moon.' This was a regular ritual whenever I visited her and it brought a sense of peace and safety to me before sleeping. It is a wonderful idea to attune children to the security of the Spirit of the Moon.

If you stand within a fairy ring (an area of grass that grows out of kilter with the surrounding grass to make a circle shape, or an area of mushrooms or daisies which are growing in a circle) and make a wish during the Full Moon, that wish should come true. It is always a good idea to collect your herbs and ingredients for spells during a New Moon for extra potency.

Wearing an amulet of the Crescent Moon, attuned to the Goddess, is an excellent way to protect yourself, but if you prefer the masculine alternative you can wear the Pair of Horns amulet which is attuned to the God and the Sun. They are both very similar in design and can be made by yourself. White daisies are often called Moon Flowers.

Below are a few basic but well worn and known spells to start you off. They have been collected from all over the world, from my own collection, ancient notes and discussions with other witches, and many from Bulgaria where Witchcraft is revered and treated with respect. They use tried and trusted ingredients and work well. Before starting a spell make absolutely sure your heart is pure and your intention is to help and serve. These are powerful tools in themselves and if you mess about or have an irreverent attitude you may conjure up more than you bargained for, or the spell may simply not work. However, the more in tune with yourself you are the easier it will become to prepare your own spells.

pertaining to mystical objects and use your talents to combine these ingredients into powerful spells of your own making.

Before you start any spell, cleanse the special place or temple you are using. This cleansing ritual will be individual to you and can take on many different styles, but it must always end with you being in the restorative state, more of which is explained later. For some examples to start with, a friend of mine always begins his ritual by saying the Lord's Prayer, possibly the most potent protection spell of all time. Another friend likes to sprinkle a strong blend of carpet cleaner over the floor

If you have the basic tools, the will to succeed and know about the best times and places to use your spells – you cannot fail. Learn about the different properties of oils and herbs, find reference books and light incense sticks and white candles to purify the air, and then thank the spirit guide that is leading her. You will know what feels right for you. I suggest lots of fresh air, at least one white candle and a prayer of thanks before you get started as your basic layout, to which you can add your own personal preferences, such as oils, flowers or sacred objects. If you have a Pentacle on your altar or table and each point is dedicated to a special name, then put an object relevant to that name on the end of each point, your sacred stone (Earth), a candle (Fire), an incense stick (Air), your chalice (Water) and a crystal (Spirit) are good examples.

When casting a spell for retribution or to return to someone the misfortune they have given out, always stand on your right leg and lift your left hand to the sky before reciting your spell. Your right leg is grounded to the earth allowing the power to move through you and your left hand lifts the spell to the elements to be borne on the wind and does not allow the negativity to remain within your body. Most important – before starting any ritual or spell, always wash your hands!

Remember that if you are under medical supervision or being treated by a doctor, or taking medication and so on, always check with them first before using any of the spells or recipes, in the rare event of allergies or the herbs not being compatible with whatever medication you may be taking.

A final thought, when spellworking your prayers must be genuine. The spirits know if someone is 'having a laugh' and at best, nothing will happen. If your desire is genuine and your prayers sincere, wonders will happen for you.

Keep in touch spell

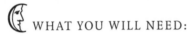

 WHAT YOU WILL NEED:

* a blue candle
* a handful of caraway seeds
* two blue pouches or small purses
* a sheet of blue paper (torn into two pieces)
* a red pen
* a snip of hair from your head and a snip from the person you want to keep in touch with

WHAT TO DO:

On a full moon, light a blue candle and sit with the person (who may be going away or whom you want to stay in touch with) within a magic circle. Hold their hands and say: '*Mother Goddess to you I pray, keep (name of person) from too far stray, keep ourselves in constant touch, Mother Goddess let it be such.*'

Then take a snip of your hair and place it in one pouch with half the caraway seeds and your name written in red on one half of the torn blue paper and give to the person. Let them snip a piece of their hair and put it in the second pouch with the remaining caraway seeds and their name written in red on the other half of the torn blue paper and give it to you. As long as you both keep these pouches on your persons, you will keep in touch. At the end of your workings, snuff out the candle (do not blow it out) and carefully remove the magic circle.

N.B. To make a magic circle for these purposes, simply sit with your friend together and draw around you in free flowing salt a circle which encompasses you both.

Spell for temporary beauty

 YOU WILL NEED:

✳ a dessert spoon of dried rose petals

✳ a dessert spoon of dried Lady's Mantle leaves

✳ large handful of dried milk powder

✳ 3 drops of oil of myrrh

✳ 2 pink candles

✳ photo or picture of beauty you would like to attain

 WHAT TO DO:

Preferably on a Friday, light the two pink candles and place one at either end of your bath. Place the picture or photo of the beauty you wish for in front of you and then run a warm bath. Firstly throw the leaves under the running water, then the petals, then the milk powder and finally the 3 drops of oil of myrrh. Get into the bath and, staring at the picture, intone: 'Dear Mother Goddess, dear Lady, bathe me in your beauteous splendour of light and bring me attraction this heavenly night.' Then wash as usual. The attraction will last for the whole day and night.

Temporary Beauty

An Egyptian spell for bringing good fortune and protection

YOU WILL NEED:

* 1 white candle
* a picture or drawing of an ear with the name Amun written in black ink underneath
* a secret place

WHAT TO DO:

Light the candle and place the drawing beneath it. Intone the ancient words, 'There is no refuge for the heart except for Amun, him-whose-name-is-secret. I speak your words aloud that all may hear of your goodness and I ask for your protection and good fortune.' Then take the paper and place in front of the candle and say, 'Proceed in peace that I may repeat to you the good deeds that my heart has done in the midst of the coiled-one in order to silence evil. I have done four good deeds in the midst of the portal of the horizon. I made the four winds that every man might breathe in his time. This is a deed thereof. I made the great flood that the poor man might have power like the great. This is a deed thereof. I made every man like his fellow, I did not command that they do evil, it is their hearts that disobey what I have said. This is a deed thereof. I made their hearts to cease forgetting the West, in order to make divine offerings to the gods of the Nomes, this is a deed thereof.' Then take the paper and place underneath the candle again and say, 'Amun, these words spoken by him whose names are secret, bless me with your protection and good fortune.' Then let the candle burn out and take the remains and the paper and throw them into a fast running stream or brook.

An Egyptian spell for the dead

YOU WILL NEED:

* a branch of vervain
* a piece of candied angelica
* a handful of earth from the side of the grave

WHAT TO DO:

To be uttered over the grave of a dear departed one whilst throwing the offerings onto the coffin, vervain first, then angelica and lastly the handful of earth. 'I call on Re-Horakhti to hear my prayer and to accept these tokens on behalf of (name of deceased). Authoritative-utterance and magic overthrow for me that one-of-evil-character, so that (name of the deceased) may see the horizon and sit in front of it. Mounds will be cities and cities will be mounds and (name of deceased) will be at everlasting peace.'

An Egyptian spell for the arrival of a letter or news

☾ YOU WILL NEED:

✳ a drawing or picture of five ears in a row with the names: *Thoth, Amenhotep, Horemheb, Ani* and *Nakhte* written, one underneath each ear in blue ink

✳ a blank piece of paper and an envelope addressed to yourself

✳ frankincense incense

✳ a place outside – high up if possible

 WHAT TO DO:

Light the incense and address the drawings of the ears as you address in turn each god, '*Dear Thoth scribal deity and lunar god, please hear my prayer. Dear Amenhotep, high steward and intermediary to Thoth, please hear my prayer. Dear Horemheb, scribe of ancient times, please hear my prayer. Dear Ani, Royal Scribe of ancient times, please hear my prayer. Dear Nakhte, scribe and patron of writers, please hear my prayer.*' Then take the envelope and waft it 5 times through the smoke of the incense and say each time, '*I wait for a letter from (name of person you are waiting to hear from), Thoth make it so.*'

Amenhotep make it so. Horemheb make it so. Ani make it so. Nakhte make it so. Thank you.' Then burn the envelope through the heat of the incense, tear it carefully into 5 pieces and scatter it on the wind. Your letter should arrive with the speed of the Ether.

An Egyptian spell for revenge

YOU WILL NEED:

* a pottery bowl
* a paint brush and some black ink
* a place close to a roadway

WHAT TO DO:

Paint the name of the person who has wronged you on the side of the bowl. Say out loud, 'I call on Ma'at, Goddess of order, balance and harmony, that she may judge the wrong-doings of (name of person) and bring me retribution.' Then take the bowl and smash it onto the ground. Sweep the remains away from you onto the road and await your justice. Be careful when smashing the bowl that fragments do not jump up and hit you or anyone near you. It may be advisable to wear protective clothing and goggles to safeguard against any accidents.

To make another take notice of you

YOU WILL NEED:

* 1 very red apple
* 1 piece of blue paper
* 1 red pen
* 1 large spoonful of liquid honey
* 3 drops of oil of heather

WHAT TO DO:

Cut off the lid of the apple in one slice. Hollow out the core of the apple, being careful not to slice through it. Write with the red pen on the blue paper the name of the one you want to notice you. Fold the paper and insert it in the hollow core of the apple. Now fill the hollow with liquid honey and 3 drops of oil of heather. Replace the lid of the apple. Now place the apple in a dark cupboard or enclosed space at the beginning of a waxing moon, until the full moon is reached. Then, on the full moon, take out the apple and bury it in your garden. If you haven't got a garden, buy a window box for this purpose – whatever you use – enclose the apple in earth. Wait for your result, which should be immediate!

If you cannot wait for the waxing moon this spell can be done at other times but you must bury the apple in earth the following day and the result may be less potent.

(The point of this spell is that you are making a sweet offering to the Goddess – the apple and honey – and at the same time drawing Her attention to your note enclosed in the offering and using colours relevant to your wish.)

To attract desire

YOU WILL NEED:

- ✳ equal parts half pint of rose water and orange blossom water
- ✳ 1 drop oil of oak
- ✳ 1 drop oil of heather
- ✳ shredded rosemary needles
- ✳ 1 drop oil of musk

WHAT TO DO:

Mix ingredients together in chalice. Leave for 14 days in a dark cool place, covered. After 14 days, take mixture and strain into a dark bottle. Wrap a green piece of tissue paper around bottle and tie with a green ribbon. Consecrate chalice on your ritual altar and light a ring of 7 pink candles around it. Pray out loud, *'To the lady of the Moon and the lord of the Sun, I ask you to bless this potion with your properties of love and desire so that as I wear it I shall attract my true love to me, with your blessing.'* Dip your middle right-hand finger in the liquid and place a drop on your 'third eye' and say *'As I wear this scent, I wear it for you, as I use this scent, my desires will be true.'* Thank and cleanse your ritual altar or table. Now wear your scent when you are near the one you wish to attract.

To rid your home of unhappy energy

☾ YOU WILL NEED:

✳ 1 old brick

✳ angelica shavings

✳ salt

✳ a chalice of cold water

☾ WHAT TO DO:

Do this spell on the first day of a waning moon. Place the brick in a hot oven for a few minutes until warmed through and hot to the touch. Take the brick out, using oven gloves or similar, and place the shredded angelica on top with the salt. Using the chalice, sprinkle the cold water over the top of the brick until steam rises and chant 7 times, 'I call on the Eye of Horus to protect this home, invasion of evil be gone to none.' When the brick has cooled, place it in front of your house outside and leave there as a warning to any other unhappy or negative energy that thinks about coming in.

For  strong hair

YOU WILL NEED:

* ✳ 1 metal comb
* ✳ chalice of warm water
* ✳ 1 teaspoon of oil of oak
* ✳ 1 teaspoon of olive oil
* ✳ the use of a horse

WHAT TO DO:

Comb the tail of the horse over your chalice of water mixed with the teaspoon of oil of oak and teaspoon of olive oil. Wash your hair in the water once a week during the waxing moon (twice in all). While doing this thank your chosen horse spirit, Epona, Mladovo, Voivoda or Kovatchite for the strength of his tail to enhance the strength of yours.

On a full moon, light a green candle with the name of the horse spirit inscribed on it and as it burns down say 7 times: 'I washed my hair and you were there, to make it strong and make it long. I washed my hair to make it fair, as you are fair please bless my hair.' Then watch the candle burn down, take a strand of hair and mould it to the candle stub and bury it in earth.

To find something lost

YOU WILL NEED:

* 1 piece of string knotted in 3 places
* 1 blue candle
* 1 white daisy

WHAT TO DO:

Light the candle, wind the string around your index finger on your left hand and hold your finger to your forehead between your eyes (your third eye). Hold the daisy in your right hand. Turn around clockwise 3 times and say: 'St Anthony, St Anthony, please return my (name of whatever's lost) to me, this daisy here is a gift to thee.' Then blow out the candle and place the candle, string and daisy on a high shelf. You should find whatever you've lost within 2 days.

For fruitfulness in all things

YOU WILL NEED:

* 7 vine stems
* your mirror
* 1 green candle
* 1 small bunch of green grapes

WHAT TO DO:

At the Spring Equinox cut 7 fresh vine stems and weave together to make a circlet for your head. At a special place to you, wearing the circlet, sit in front of your mirror and light a green candle with the name Triffon inscribed in the wax. Place a bunch of green grapes around the base of the candle. Look into the mirror at the space over your right shoulder. Relax and keep staring. The moment Triffon shows himself to you in whatever form, thank him aloud for listening to your request and proceed to convey your need for fruitfulness. At the end of your request, thank him again and blow out the candle. Place the unlit candle and grapes somewhere high up in your house and leave there for one month. Then bury them in earth.

114

To make a wish come true

YOU WILL NEED:

* onion skins
* 5 drops of oil of frankincense
* chalice of water collected from a running waterfall

WHAT TO DO:

Do this spell on the first day of a waxing moon. Take the onion skins and soak them in your chalice with the 5 drops of oil and water for 1 day. Then take the soaked skins and dry them for a further 2 days in the heat of the sun. On the fourth day, in the morning, set fire to the onion skins in a safe place, preferably outside, or in a hearth, and concentrate on your wish. Intone, 'I ask the Sun God and the Goddess of the Moon to grant my wish, (repeat wish), the roasted skins my offering to the great fire, the fruit my offering to the great light, as the Moon waxes, so will the power of this wish, let it be done in thy two great names.'

To protect yourself before venturing out

YOU WILL NEED:

✳ a glass of cold water

WHAT TO DO:

Before stepping outside your home, open the front door and throw the glass of water onto the floor directly outside. As you step outside say aloud, '*May all my (or your) problems go with the water, Lord and Lady bless my steps.*' Make sure you tread in the water as you move away from your home. (Do not turn back into your home at the same time as this will reverse the spell.)

For general good luck and fortune

 YOU WILL NEED:

* a necklace made of plaited vervain herb
* 1 chicken's egg
* red paint
* a garden or window box

WHAT TO DO:

Do this spell at 1 o'clock on the first day of spring. Plait and wear the vervain herb as a garland around your neck. Boil the egg for 10 minutes. Take it out and let it cool then paint it red. Bury it in your garden or windowbox and leave the vervain necklace on top.

To encourage fertility

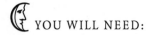

YOU WILL NEED:

* leaves and flowers of the herb Lady's Mantle
* distilled water
* 1 rattle
* a handful of oak leaves
* 1 green candle
* a handful of walnuts
* a place sacred to you

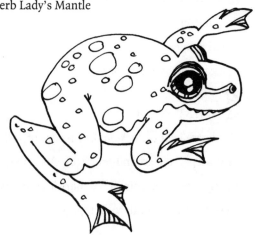

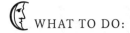

WHAT TO DO:

Make a decoction tea with the
herb Lady's Mantle and
distilled water and drink every
day for 3 weeks. (To make a
decoction place 50g of dried plant
in a litre of distilled water, soak for an
hour, then bring to the boil and infuse for 10
minutes.) Also put the flowers and leaves of Lady's Mantle in your bath. After
3 weeks, take the rest of the ingredients and put half of the walnuts with the
rattle and place under some leaves in an area sacred to you, preferably
outside. Light the candle and sit it on top of the leaves. Relax in front of your
offering and slowly eat the remaining walnuts whilst thinking of your
particular fertility needs, call on *Imhotep* for his help with your fertility
problems. When the candle has burned down, leave it and walk around the
pile deozil-wise (clockwise) 3 times. Say the words that come to your mind
asserting your wish for success in this matter. Leave your offering where it is.

To Find out whether your lover is true

YOU WILL NEED:

* 1 hazelnut
* 1 blue pen
* 1 piece of red paper
* a bonfire

WHAT TO DO:

Write the name of your lover in blue pen on the red paper and wrap it around the hazelnut. Place it at the edge of the bonfire and watch closely. If the nut burns slowly, all is well. If the nut jumps about, flares or explodes there is a strong possibility your lover has some explaining to do!

Magic massage oil

YOU WILL NEED:

✳ a good handful of fresh rosemary

✳ almond oil to cover the herbs

✳ 2 drops of oil of lavender

✳ a good handful of fresh goutweed (ground elder) leaves

✳ a large jug of spring or holy water (this can be from your Altar or a church if you prefer).

WHAT TO DO:

Crush the goutweed leaves with a pestle and cover with holy water in your cauldron. Bring to the boil then simmer for 10 minutes. Add this mixture to the rest of the ingredients in a covered pot. Shake well and place in a cool, dark area for 2 weeks, shaking every day. Then strain the liquid into a dark coloured bottle and take to your temple and place on the altar. Ask the Lord and Lady to give their blessings to this oil and energize it with their healing power. Light a green candle and pray to Nature's healing spirits to protect and vitalize this gift. Thank the Lord and Lady for listening and close your spellworking in your usual manner. The oil should last for up to 3 months.

Sleep safe

 YOU WILL NEED:

✳ 3 onions chopped
✳ 1 pint of water
✳ butter
✳ 1 cup of valerian tea

 WHAT TO DO:

This can only be used as a medicinal soup and should be taken immediately – it cannot be stored for future use!

Stew the onions in the butter gently and then add the pint of water and 1 cup of valerian tea. Bubble in cauldron for at least half an hour then, when the onions are soft, liquidize. Transfer to a bowl and serve with a slice of plain brown bread and give to the afflicted. Sit in your temple while the soup is being eaten, light a white candle and say: 'Power of the Moon and Sun please bless this spell that I have done, allow the sleepsafe to begin and cleanse the mind of troubles within. Sleepsafe dear your mind is clear.' Blow out the candle and cleanse the temple.

Travel protector

☾ YOU WILL NEED:

* 3 pints of water
* half a tablespoon of ammonia
* 5 shreds of ginseng
* 2 drops of lavender

☾ WHAT TO DO:

Mix all the ingredients together in your cauldron. Pray to the God and Goddess asking them to use their hands to lift you safely whilst travelling. After asking the God and Goddess' blessing on your travel protector, and ritually cleansing your spell, sprinkle the potion on your suitcases or bags before travelling and then wash your feet in the remaining water. Empty the water, preferably in your garden or windowbox, and as it sinks into the Earth (or if necessary, the sink), say *'This water I have washed in is now returned safely to Mother Earth and so shall I safely travel and return.'*

Not for internal use.

Travel future

YOU WILL NEED:

* Aquarian incense
* 1 stick lemon grass
* caraway seeds

WHAT TO DO:

Cut lemon grass into shreds and dry thoroughly. Mix grass and caraway seeds together and sprinkle over your empty suitcase. In your temple, light the incense on your altar and meditate on the places you wish to travel to. Pray to Gabriel to take you over the water, pray to Auriel to take you over the earth, pray to Raphael to breathe life into your plans and pray to Michael to ignite with success and safety your travel plans. Thank the God and Goddess for listening and close your spellworking.

For success in a business deal

(C YOU WILL NEED:

* thyme incense
* 3 fresh basil leaves
* 3 fresh dill leaves
* a branch of vervain herb

(C WHAT TO DO:

The night before your business deal, sit within a magic circle and light the thyme incense. Take the basil leaves and place them in front of you in a line and then cover each leaf with a dill leaf to form a cross shape. Take the vervain branch and pass it through the incense and then touch one of the leaves, then pass it through the incense and touch the next leaf, then again for the third leaf. As you pass the vervain branch through the incense, say each time, *'magical wheel take this business deal'* then when you touch the dill and basil crosses say each time, *'basil of hate, abate, dill bring good will to this business deal'*. When you have done this three times, eat the basil and dill leaves and take the vervain branch and pass it again through the incense and say: '*Mother make it so, let my business deal grow. Lady be kind, make my business deal bind. Spirit of the Moon, grant me this boon.*' Stay within the circle until the incense has burned out and then say a ritual prayer of thanks and protection and close the workings.

Financial future

YOU WILL NEED:

* one gold candle
* Witches' knife (Athame)
* oil of frankincense
* 2 pieces of straw

WHAT TO DO:

On the first day of a waxing moon inscribe the name of your God and Goddess down two sides of the candle with your Witches' knife. Place the 2 pieces of straw on your altar in an exact cross shape and place your candle on top of the straw. Drip 3 drops of oil of frankincense on the top of the candle and light it. Whilst it is burning pray for your

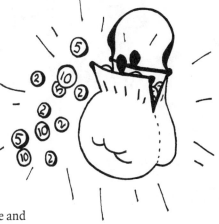

financial future and ask the God of the Sun and the Goddess of the Moon to help you achieve the finances you need. Concentrate and meditate on the areas you need help with concerning finances, put out the candle with a snuffer and continue the same instructions every day of the waxing moon up until full moon. When the candle has burned down to a stub, keep it with the straw in your purse or wallet where it should attract financial success to you.

Love potion – to attract affection

YOU WILL NEED:

✳ 50g of dried wild pansy or Heartsease
✳ 1 litre of water
✳ 3 drops of neroli oil
✳ 2 drops of sandalwood
✳ 1 warm bath

WHAT TO DO:

Soak the wild pansy in the litre of water for 3 hours and then bring to the boil in your cauldron. When cooled, add the neroli oil and sandalwood to the mixture and bath in the recipe every day for a week starting at the beginning of a waxing moon. If you wish to attract affection from a particular person, mention his or her particular name to the God and Goddess in your temple while blessing the potion and asking that it only be so if it is their will. You should receive a sign by the end of the following week.

Love potion – to dispel unwanted affection

 YOU WILL NEED:

* dried camphor leaves
* salt
* handful of chopped, dried lemonbalm
* vodka
* an item or symbol of the unwanted affection
* your broomstick

 WHAT TO DO:

Cover the camphor and lemonbalm with the vodka, sprinkle a few grains of salt and leave for one week in a dark place. Take the object symbolizing the unwanted affection (for example a photo, the name, etc) and place it outside your front door. Sprinkle the potion on top of the object and say, '*Like the camphor dispells moths, so my potion dispells your affection, leave me in peace and return to your own happiness.*' As the last drops of the potion saturate the object, take your broomstick and literally sweep the object away from your front door.

A recipe to aid peace of mind

 YOU WILL NEED:

✳ 4 green peppers

✳ 1 cucumber

✳ olive oil

✳ 1 block of feta cheese

✳ 1 oz finely chopped parsley

 WHAT TO DO:

Cut the heads off the peppers and scrape out the seeds inside without ruining the shape of the pepper. Roast under the grill until skin blackens. Skin the peppers, leaving as whole as possible. Peel and chop the cucumber, mix with the parsley, feta cheese and stuff into the peppers. Sprinkle olive oil over the peppers and leave in the fridge. Eat slowly when you are feeling low or need peace of mind. Concentrate on the flavours, the sweetness of the peppers, the freshness of the parsley and watch your mood lift itself and your mind calm.

A recipe to aid revitalization of humours!

 **YOU WILL NEED:**

* 1 large pot of organic natural yoghurt
* 2 equal pot sizes of water
* 1 cucumber
* 2oz/50g/½ cup crushed walnuts
* 1 teaspoon olive oil
* parsley
* salt
* 1 clove of garlic

WHAT TO DO:

Mix the yoghurt and water together to form a thin liquid. Add the finely chopped cucumber, walnuts, grated garlic, oil, parsley and salt to taste. Blend all ingredients to form a smooth drinkable consistency. Drink as a cold soup with a spoon and you should feel immediately uplifted.

A recipe for love biscuits

YOU WILL NEED:

* 8oz/225g/ 1 cup butter
* 4oz/125g/½ cup caster sugar
* 3 drops of rose oil
* 12oz/350g/2 ¼ cups plain flour
* 3oz/75g/½ cup icing sugar
* candied borage flowers

WHAT TO DO:

Melt the butter and leave to cool and set. Then beat the butter with a wooden spoon until it goes white. Add the caster sugar and beat for another 15 minutes, add the flour and 3 drops of rose oil to form a dough mixture. Form the dough mixture into your lover's initials, love hearts, etc. Cook at a low temperature 150°C (300°F/Gas Mark 2) for approximately half an hour. The biscuits should stay white, remove them just before they start to brown. When cooked and cooled, place a candied borage flower on each one and dust liberally with icing sugar.

A recipe for love plums

☾ YOU WILL NEED:

* 2lb/450g/ripe plums
* 4oz/125g/½ cup brown sugar
* 1 stick cinnamon
* grated rind of 1 lemon
* grated rind of 1 orange
* grated rind of 1 lime
* 4 fl oz Marsala wine
* 2 fl oz plum or cherry brandy

☾ WHAT TO DO:

Cut the plums to remove the stones. Place in cauldron with the sugar, cinnamon and lemon, orange and lime rind. Pour the Marsala wine over, cover and stew gently for approximately one hour until the plums are soft. Add the brandy and mix into the plums. Serve immediately with the love biscuits.

A recipe for the removal of skin complaints

WHAT TO DO:

Mix ingredients together and leave for 21 days in a cool dark place, high up and not exposed to the air. Turn container each day and finally drain liquid into a dark bottle. Bless and cast a ritual spell of your own over this oil and empower it with the ability to remove skin problems, such as spots, dry skin, stretch marks, etc. Massage onto afflicted areas of unbroken skin only and do not use on your face.

YOU WILL NEED:

* fresh marigolds, washed and dried
* sunflower oil to cover flowers
* 1 tbsp of almond oil
* a bunch of parsley or Salad Burnet

A recipe for the removal of freckles

🌙 YOU WILL NEED:

✳ 5 chopped fresh yarrow leaves

✳ 1 litre of spring water

✳ grated horseradish root

🌙 WHAT TO DO:

Mix the yarrow and grated
horseradish root with 1 litre of
spring water. Bring to the boil and
simmer for 20 minutes. Drain and
leave to cool. Keep in a dark place
and apply sparingly to freckles.

A recipe for problem skin

☾ YOU WILL NEED:

✴ 1 cup of chopped periwinkle
leaves

✴ 1 cup of rosewater

✴ 1 crushed leaf of the vervain plant

✴ ½ cup of white lard

☾ WHAT TO DO:

Mix the ingredients including the lard in your cauldron. Very slowly bring to boiling point and then remove from heat to cool. Apply the lotion as a cleanser over the problem skin and leave on skin for half an hour. Then rinse skin firstly with warm water and then with cold water. Not to be taken internally. Keep applying for as long as it takes.

To wish upon the moon spell

YOU WILL NEED:

* your magic scrying mirror
* a white candle
* a piece of paper with your wish written on it
* a full moon

WHAT TO DO:

Go outside, light the white candle and look at the moon's reflection in your scrying mirror. While holding the wish at the back of the mirror say 7 times: 'Goddess of the Moon these words are true, grant me this wish as I believe in you.' All the time focusing on the moon's reflection. Then take the paper wish and burn it in the candle flame. Take the candle stub when it has burned out and carry it in your pocket at the time when you want your wish to come true. After that, bury the candle stub in earth.

To wish upon a star spell

YOU WILL NEED:

✳ your magic wand

✳ a silver candle

✳ a piece of white paper with your wish written on it

✳ a clear night with the stars visible

WHAT TO DO:

Go outside and raise your magic wand to the star that shines brightest and incant 3 times, 'Starbright and Starlight, grant my wish with love tonight.' Then light your candle and burn the paper wish in the flame of the candle letting the ashes scatter around you. Finally, raise your wand to the star and say loudly 'So be it.'

Wish
Upon
a
Star

Menus for the sabbats

☆ Yule Sabbat ☆

 CELEBRATING THE BIRTH OF GOD

✳ Holly, ivy and mistletoe to decorate

✳ White, red and gold candles

✳ Frankincense, myrrh and gold incense

 MENU

✳ Potato and carrot soup

✳ Roast turkey, roast potatoes, roast parsnips,

sprouts with chestnuts, peas with bacon

✳ Caraway bread or rolls

✳ Fruitcake, Christmas pudding, brandy butter and assorted nuts

✳ Oranges in brandy

☆ Imbolg Sabbat ☆

 CELEBRATING REJUVENATION

* Snowdrops
* Green leaves to decorate
* Yellow, green and blue candles
* Lavender, jasmine and lemon incense

MENU

* Ratatouille made of pumpkins, marrow, tomatoes, courgettes, mushrooms, onions and peppers and scattered with grated cheddar cheese and pine kernals
* Sesame seed bread
* Seedicake
* Blackberry or rosehip tea
* Sparkling wine

☆ Ostara Sabbat ☆

☾ CELEBRATING PROCREATION

✳ Daffodils, crocus and

   tulips to decorate

✳ Purple and pink candles

✳ Ginger, patchouli and incense

☾ MENU

✳ Herb stuffed hard-boiled eggs with mayonnaise

✳ Pancakes with lemon and sugar

✳ Love Plums and Love Biscuits (see recipes,

   pages 132 & 133)

✳ Honey and grapes

☆ Beltane Sabbat ☆

🌙 CELEBRATING FERTILITY AND HEALING

✳ Ivy, hawthorne blossom, Lady's Mantle
   flowers and leaves and red roses to decorate
✳ Red and pink candles
✳ Rosemary, pansy, basil, sweet
   almond and sandalwood incense

🌙 MENU

✳ Oatmeal biscuits
✳ Beetroot salad
✳ Fish
✳ Red apples, cherries, strawberries,
   raspberries and plums
✳ Pink Cava, barley wine

☆ Litha Sabbat ☆

CELEBRATING LOVE AND HEALTH POWER

- ✳ Mint, honeysuckle and roses to decorate
- ✳ White, red, blue and green candles
- ✳ Summer, Air and Water incense

MENU

- ✳ Various breads and cheeses
- ✳ Salads such as coleslaw and waldorf
- ✳ Cherry pie and cream
- ✳ Lemon meringue pie
- ✳ Watermelon, beer and still water

☆ Lammas Sabbat ☆

 CELEBRATING CREATION AND TRANSFORMATION

* Wheat, corn and apples to decorate
* Brown, white and yellow candles
* Heather, oak and musk incense

MENU

* Lamb and rice dishes
* Spinach
* Brown or wholemeal bread
* Hazelnuts
* Elderflower champagne, beer

☆ Mabon Sabbat ☆

🌙 CELEBRATING RENEWAL AND REST

* Dark foliage and
  grapes to decorate
* Silver, white and green
  candles
* Sandalwood and juniper
  incense

🌙 MENU

* Wheaten bread,
  croissants and butter
* Nut cutlets with peas
  and sweetcorn
* Apple pie
* Cider
* Sparkling water

☆ Samhain Sabbat ☆

 CELEBRATING REINCARNATION AND COMMUNION
   WITH DEAD SPIRITS

✳ Hollowed out pumpkins, cobwebs and Egyptian artifacts to decorate

✳ Silver, black, aquamarine and purple candles

✳ Peppermint, musk and orange incense

MENU

✳ Pumpkin soup

✳ Crumpets, soft rolls

✳ Chocolate offerings for departed spirits

✳ Jacket potatoes and cheese

✳ Bean stew

✳ Herbal tea, red wine and port

For all menus, tofu and Quorn can be substituted for meat. Soya milk
products can be substituted for full milk products.

❛... And I?

I was gone

Away with the swirling leaves

of Autumn...❜

Book of Souls – Akashic Records

⭐ CLIENTS AND MYSTICAL
SPECIALITIES

Clients

A Client is a modern word for the people or forces that need your help. A true Witch should never charge an exact sum for their services, but should say that whatever the client feels is appropriate, should be given. Remember, if the client is unsatisfied with the help then they can just as easily donate nothing at all and that is perfectly acceptable.

In ancient days the norm was to give the Witch a present such as a chicken or some vegetables – whatever the client produced or had to hand. Witchcraft is not about making money, but a good Witch can usually survive quite happily on the proceeds of her work. Money is not the abiding object here, it is about doing good wherever possible and helping people. If you keep that in your mind at all times, your success will be assured.

Established Witches usually rely on word of mouth. When someone is happy with the results they will often go away and tell someone else and so the chain develops. However, when you are first starting out it can be difficult to let people know about your talents.

Of course you may not want clients but prefer to practise your magic alone and for your house only, which is perfectly acceptable. Although be assured, once the swirls of magical energy get going, people cannot help but notice and be drawn to you!

If you want to advertise your services as a White Witch there are many simple options to start you off. You could put an advertisement in a local paper, go along to one of the psychic fairs, subscribe to psychic magazines and scour their contacts pages for like-minded people. If you feel it is not going to be detrimental to you, tell your friends, at work or at play – word of mouth is always a fast communication tool! Perhaps you could convince your local health shop, surgery or café to put up an advertisement about your services! Look on the Internet and in libraries. Whatever you do, before you do it, cast a spell for success and you will be sure to succeed! If you pray to the God and Goddess for their support and your intention is purely honourable, you will be amazed at the quickness of their reply and how readily they will help you.

Mystical Specialities

Witches have their own areas of mysticality that they specialize in. My particular specialities range from tea and coffee reading to the I Ching (an ancient Chinese form of foretelling future events and answers to important questions). You probably feel more drawn towards a particular area of mysticality than other areas and as such you should follow your instincts and read up all you can about your particular interest. There are so many wonderful reference books around, especially in libraries. Psychic fairs are abounding these days, Witches and Seers are in every town, look in papers, magazines, phone books! If you **want to find out you will find out,** and remember to practise at all times so that your skills can grow and develop. Here are a few areas you might be interested in developing your skills:

Palmistry, Runes, Omens, Tarot, I Ching, Handwriting, Mind Magic, Spirit Channelling, Numerology, Reading tea-leaves or coffee-grounds, Astronomy, Astrology, Crystal Healing, Spellworking, Scrying, Dowsing, Meditation, Pathworking, Aromatherapy, Remote Viewing, Hands-on healing, Autonomic writing, Akashic Records and Astral travel, to name but a few. Whatever your particular pull is, it is special to you, so believe in yourself and your powers. If you persevere success is assured!

Mind Magic

Mind magic is exactly what it sounds like: creating magic with the power of your mind. As everyone seems to know nowadays we do not use the whole of our brain, only a small percentage, and if we can tap into the unused area, we can find our magic powers. It is not an easy thing to do and requires a lot of practice, but if you persevere you will slowly find yourself more and more able to access parts of your brain that have remained dormant for a long time.

There are many examples of the use your magic power can be to you and others through simply tuning into your untapped mental energy. For example, using the magic power

of your psyche to heal, to astral travel, to turn off pain, to keep yourself healthy, to appeal to others so that good results appear, to contact people through the Ether, to make yourself invisible, to communicate to animals, and so on and so on – in short, to make things HAPPEN!

Once you have tuned in to your particular Mind Magic, you have a responsibility to use it with care and only for the good of yourself or others. This is a very powerful area of magic and has dramatic results and you should recognize that and treat your gifts with caution and respect.

STAGE ONE

⭐

Accessing your Mind Magic

To start to access your Mind Magic, the first thing you must do is find a place to concentrate where you will not be disturbed, for example, your temple of worship, the garden or perhaps your bedroom. Sit or lie in a position that is most comfortable for you and breathe in and out, concentrating on your breathing and counting one, two, for each breath you take in and out. You may close your eyes if this helps. As you relax, you should aim to slowly lose all awareness of the space around you and begin to concentrate on a ball of healing white light that rises from your stomach and slowly starts to move around your body, casting a glow of healing, restorative power throughout you as it covers every inch of your body and then returns to your stomach area, having cast a web of white healing power around your body.

When you are ready to return to reality, simply feel the ball of white power return within yourself and slowly return back to your counting and concentrating on your breathing. The surroundings then begin to appear around you and you become more conscious and then fully awake and full of restorative power.

This is Stage One of the exercise and it is important to practise in order to relax and reach a meditative and protective state. This should be practised as often as you feel comfortable until you have the ability to restore yourself at will wherever you are and whatever your situation.

STAGE TWO

The Restorative State

When you are in your relaxed state with the ball of white restorative power having spun its web and now hovering over your stomach area – you can begin to concentrate on the area you are most interested in accessing, for example, healing another that may be some distance from you or communicating through your mind to contact another. After you have finished in your particular area, always return back to the white restorative ball of power and slowly count yourself back to reality.

Communication with Others

If you need to communicate with someone and do not know their whereabouts, or if they are on a different plane, lie or sit down and imagine a picture of the person you are trying to communicate with. As the picture becomes clearer, create a scenario where they suddenly think of you, concentrate on them becoming aware that they need to contact you and make your picture of them move towards a telephone or fax or writing paper. You are in control of this situation and by carefully concentrating on the person and sending your thought waves to them, requesting contact, you will see them start to move and understand that they need to contact you.

If the person in question is on a different plane, instead of writing or telephoning you must concentrate on talking to them, then and there. As you relax and concentrate, they will begin to answer you. If your thought waves are particularly strong you may be able to have a conversation with a person on the same plane as you – although be aware this takes some practice.

Healing Powers

Healing yourself and healing others are two different skills, which each require different powers and are used in different ways. If you need to heal yourself, you must do this when in your restorative state (above); to heal others you need to tune in to your magic abilities while you are in a conscious state. However sending healing thoughts while you are in your restorative state is an extra bonus to one who needs it.

To heal yourself

There are many different ways to learn to heal yourself but when you are starting out it is best to have a simple meditative visualization to concentrate on in order to channel the healing energy. Once you have accomplished success with the positive thought process it is then more natural to move on to more intense ways to heal.

Firstly, access your restorative state, then visualize the white light turning green – a soft, glowing green full of healthy energy, pulsating with nature's forces and a natural energy attuned to the Earth – which travels over your body and concentrates on the areas that are out of line and causing you pain. Slowly watch the green light change into a cool, blue healing energy which beams its healing powers straight to the root of the problem, cools the area and starts regenerating the area. Then follow the blue light as it changes to a warm golden glow which covers the blue healing with an energizing, vitalized healing light full of the Earth's energy. When you feel comfortable and healthy, watch the golden light change back into the restorative white light. Do this exercise every night for as long as it takes.

To heal others

Wherever you are and whoever your patient is, be it animal, plant or human, concentrate on using the white restorative power within you to combine with the strength and vitality in your patient. You will find your own way – some people like to lay their hands on the patient, others use the energy from a distance – but whichever you prefer, concentrate on the healing energy within you and feel it travel through your body as a bolt of electricity into the patient; using the power of your mind watch it heal the patient and know that the energy is doing good.

Feel yourself tune in to the Earth energy, Chi or Prana and become part of the cosmos. While you are doing this be aware that the restorative power is not only connected to you but also connected to the patient, so your thoughts and prayers of healing and positive energy are transmuted to them. Always call on the Goddess to bless your healing in the name of love. This will take time and effort. Some people feel the energy as a form of heat, others see it as a light. Your own will will determine how your healing process develops, but concentrate at all times on the good you are doing for another and use your prayers to the Goddess to ask for her support in your endeavours.

Akashic Records

Someone once told me that the best way to imagine the Akashic Records is to visualize the Library of the Universe in Heaven. The Akashic Records are all the records in Heaven and Earth and contain all the information in the Universe! That is quite a deep thing to visualize, so if you imagine a library which goes on forever, that is a good start!

You visit the Akashic Records by meditating and entering your trance-like state. Slowly visualizing a door is always a good way to start, as the door is your entrance to the spirit world as well as the way back. Once through the door you see rows upon rows upon rows of books. You walk slowly towards one of the shelves where you visualize one of the books drawing you to it. Reach out in your mind and take the book off the shelf. Try to read its cover, open its pages and read its contents. This takes a lot of practice so don't despair if you can't do it immediately! It is highly unlikely for anyone to immediately grasp this technique, as it requires great concentration, skill and relaxation. Touch the book, can you feel what it is made of? Smell the book, does it smell musty? New? Listen to yourself rustling the pages of the book, are they thick pages or thin? Does the book weigh a lot or is it very light? Think and meditate on all these things to bring the book into your consciousness. Eventually, with practice, you will be able to read the book. The next step is to write down what you read for your future reference. The gifts within the Akashic Records are monumental and should be treated with respect and reverence and utter secrecy, but if you have trained yourself this far, you will probably know that already!

Astral Travel

This is the means to travel all over the cosmos by using the power of your mind, and connected to your spiritual cord. By intense meditation, through sleep and practice, your spiritual self can leave your body and journey wherever it wants.

The spiritual cord is a shimmering line of energy that winds itself endlessly from your soul to the place your body is resting and travelling from, thereby keeping you safe whilst you travel. The cord is so strong it should not be broken and if you feel you need to return to your body at any time you can do so by following the cord home. You can cover great distances and see great sights and learn many things but, as in all things magical, it requires self-restraint, practice and sensibility before it can be achieved. Having said that, many people, myself included, have experienced astral travel in earlier years without even trying, which can be quite an experience and is usually the way people start to investigate more about it.

To start your practice, lie in bed or on the floor in your temple (again somewhere you won't be disturbed), close your eyes and ask the God and Goddess to protect you on your travels. Concentrate on your

breathing and feel the air from your
nostrils as it touches the top of your
lip, now start to feel yourself
floating. Concentrate on the
sensation of pushing down
with your body while
your soul lifts
upwards at the same
time, then change to
pushing down with
your soul and up with
your body. It is like
imagining a separation
of two halves, one
half going up at
the same time as
the other half goes
down. Eventually it
becomes a see-saw

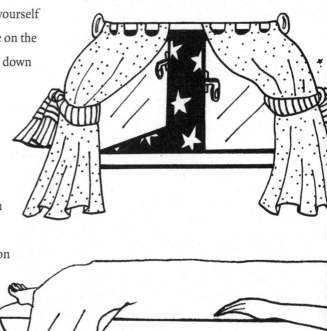

sensation and you should become more aware of literally moving, usually upwards. Sometimes it works like a spiral, where you slowly start to rotate and then start moving upwards. Relax and enjoy the sensation and as you do so try to see the shimmering silver or golden cord that is allowing you to leave your body in its resting place and – attached to your spirit self – move you gently in whichever direction you want to go. Think about where you want to visit and with practice you will begin to see many things. If you particularly want to visit someone, keep their mental image in your mind, imagine their home or place they will be and go there. You can do it!

When winding back do so slowly and peacefully, enjoying the sensation of returning to your physical body. When grounded place your hand on the floor and thank the God and Goddess for your experience, and for returning you safely. Sleep well.

Visualization Techniques

Visualization is very important when you are meditating or spellworking. Like all things, it takes practice, although you may find you are creatively inspired because of the person you are. Practice on seeing pictures in the mind, allow them to flow and change shape, and when a particular object seems sharp enough, hone in on it and practice looking at its detail, colour and texture. Sometimes the more you concentrate, the more the pictures elude you, so try and remain relaxed and positive and eventually it should become second nature and an eighth sense!

Temple and Shrine in the Ether

This is based on the above visualization technique but where you progress to creating a room for your magical workings in your mind. This can be your temple or a shrine to the God and Goddess, whichever is easiest to start off with.

Imagine a square, white, empty room hanging in the Ether. Walk about it, hear your footsteps echoing (there are no carpets!), touch the newly painted walls, smell the clean air and associate yourself totally with this room. Then, in time, slowly add the pieces of equipment and furniture that you require to dress the room with. Always be aware of the door which takes you in and out of your room. You can use your room for spellworking or simply relaxing, the great thing about it is that you can conjure it up whenever and wherever you are! The more you visit your room, the more you will recognize it, and its picture should not change unless you decide to change it. It is your safety-net and special place which goes with you everywhere.

Animal Communication

Some people are more prone to animal communication than others and they know instinctively if they are or not. Animals are usually drawn to them, they may own many animals and whenever possible talk to animals as a natural instinct rather than putting on a show. The great thing is when animals begin to respond and talk back!

Animals do not use the English language but their means of

communication is one you can recognize and understand, the same as French or Italian if you have been learning it! Animals can tell us a lot and if you have a Familiar or

167

Famulus you are blessed! The best way to learn how to communicate is simply by talking to your animal on a regular basis. They may not immediately talk back, although they often do with particular sound-noises that mean different things. Animals are very sensitive to your vibrations, so if you can induce feelings of love and affection while you are talking the animal will respond. Similarly, if you induce feelings of anger or sorrow, the animal will respond back to you in a completely different way. As you practice asking questions of your animal, giving suggestions, praising and simply chatting, you will slowly start to recognize the different variations in your animal's responses and thereby learn its language. Once you've achieved this, it's quite easy to pick up a total communication skill with your animal. My cat is extraordinarily easy to chat to; she often closes the cupboard door after I've taken out her plate to feed her. This always makes me laugh!

Making Yourself Invisible to Others

In this nightmare world of communication and travel we have rather overextended ourselves. A lot of people are suffering from stress and depression and it is because our senses have become overloaded. Making yourself invisible is simply a way to cut out all the noise and confusion and to allow yourself to travel about in anonymity. The obvious ways to become anonymous are to turn off the phone, draw the curtains, stay in bed – but these are hardly useful if you have a pressing need to visit your supermarket or go to work! So, what do you do?

Firstly you should dress in the colours of shadows: grey, black, touches of white, brown; then you comb your hair (if you have hair) around your face and keep your head and your eyes down. When you walk outside, keep next to walls and on the outside edges of things, such as crowds, queues, etc. Do not look at anyone in the face, concentrate on their legs and the lower half of buildings, but use your sense of hearing to warn you of your whereabouts. Obviously you will need to look up if you are crossing a road or something similarly dangerous – but I am talking about your general walking routes. Concentrate on being invisible and you will become invisible. If all else fails, umbrellas are good hiding sticks, and large hats and sunglasses in the summer!

Funnily enough, although some people think that if you wear sunglasses you attract attention, the opposite is true – because your eyes

(the window of the soul) cannot be seen. Although people may look at you initially, they will not hold the gaze. They cannot see your eyes, but they know that you can see them, thus you have the advantage, which makes people uncomfortable, so they look away. Sunglasses are a way of telling people to ignore you!

People do not tend to stare at others unless they particularly stand out. If you have dressed inconspicuously and do not catch their eye, they will not see you, being too preoccupied with their own thoughts. There are literal ways to become invisible, strange as it may sound, but these require virtually a lifetime's dedication to learning the art and only some people have the knack! The secret is again in the use of the powers of the mind and using concentration, meditation, fasting and secret spells in order to change your physical being to a spiritual atomic being, thus enabling you to hang around in a different dimension while still being in this one. As well as all this hard work, you then have to find the way to deflect light from your appearance, (which is made up of light) and bounce the light rays back so that you become invisible. However, for the first time Witch, these abilities are a touch advanced to look into and should only be attempted when one has reached the required stage. You will know when you are there. In the meantime, concentrate on blending in like a chameleon and you will find positive results immediately.

To Restore Your Youth

Each one of us is different and some are luckier than others when it comes to our appearance. If you have inherited bad skin you will need to take more care than someone who has inherited clear, smooth skin! However, the basic premise is the same: water within and protection without.

When it comes to natural beauty the most important aspect to remember is to drink lots of natural water which will cleanse your inner body and keep your skin supple. Protect the outside layers of your skin from too much exposure to the sun by cleansing carefully, moisturizing daily. Keep your thoughts happy and exercise your facial muscles every day. Gentle exercise such as walking and stretching exercises increase the oxygen in the body, which is a youth restorer. Take plenty of vitamin C. Dab surgical spirit mixed with water on any spots (but do not use too much as it is very strong!) or use witch hazel gel. A good toner will stimulate the skin cells and keep the skin taut. Using it every day will cleanse your skin in the most refreshing and suitable way and keep it looking young. White, sparkling eye shadow or cream used sparingly under the lower eyelashes make your eyes appear larger and younger. There are marvellous creams around these days, which include the property pro-Retinol A, which alleviates particularly heavy lines that appear on the face.

On top of all this sound practical advice, regular prayer at your altar will continue your youth – as long as the emphasis is on health as opposed to vanity! Sleep is a great restorative, and also meditation, so make sure you get plenty of that. If you can, visualize a fountain of youth water splashing into a clear pool, high up on a mountain which you visit on the spiritual plane; take a daily swim in the pool and see how the fountain of youth restores you.

Ultimately, the ingestion of organic natural bio yoghurt, containing the Bulgarian bacteria and fresh organic chives, on a daily basis is said to increase your lifespan. Angelica is believed to be an elixir and a tea made from the leaves of the angelica plant is an

excellent nerve tonic. However, angelica must NOT be taken by diabetics due to its natural sugar and diuretic properties. Shitake mushrooms strengthen the immune system. Of course, there are marvellous vitamins and herb extracts widely available that support the body's structure far longer than in the past. The ultimate advice that has always been given for long life is: Everything in moderation! Scientists are fast discovering amazing results with experiments into gene manipulation renewal, stem cell regeneration and DNA engineering too, so there is every possibility that if you hold on for long enough, if necessary, science will be able to take over!

174

Witches' Basics
A Basic Shopping List for Spellworking

* Herbs
* Oils
* Coloured paper and
  coloured pens
* String or ribbons
* Candles
* Incense
* Earth
* Salt – mysteries
* Wine – spirit
* Pestle and mortar

* Your magic tools
* This book

☆ General Herbs and Foods used in Healing ☆

✳ Angelica – for protection and colds (not to be used by diabetics)

✳ Camphor – to expel moths and other unsavoury senses

✳ Garlic – for blood, indigestion, bad dreams and poor circulation

✳ Salt water – for cleansing a wound

✳ Oil of cloves – for toothache

✳ Shitake mushrooms – to boost the immune system

✳ Elecampine roots – gargle to tighten the gums

✳ Peppermint tea – aids digestion

✳ Rosemary – to improve the memory and for happiness

✳ Linden or lime leaves – to aid digestion and calm nerves

✳ Sage – remedy for colds and as a general tonic for good

✳ Chicory – for fright

✳ Goat's-rue (french lilac) – for foot wash

✳ Oil of oak – for exhaustion

✳ Olives – after recovering from an illness

✳ Walnuts – for fertility problems and menopause

- ✳ Oats – to cleanse the body and clear the mind
- ✳ Camomile tea – for stress
- ✳ Raw cabbage and carrots – for boosting the immune system
- ✳ Oil of lavender – to clear the mind of worries and stress
- ✳ Parsley – for piles and freckles
- ✳ Woad – a dye plant for colour
- ✳ Orris – a fixative for scent
- ✳ Thyme – for coughs
- ✳ Radish juice – for removal of warts
- ✳ Organic natural yoghurt – to aid longevity
- ✳ Cider vinegar in water – to cleanse the skin from impurities
- ✳ Bananas – for happiness
- ✳ Powdered pectin, one teaspoon mixed in honey – for upset stomachs
- ✳ Green tea – for peace of mind
- ✳ Sweetcorn, wholemeal bread and baked beans – for constipation
- ✳ Spinach – for fatigue

Protection Symbols

★ Eye of Horus (Udjat) ★

The Udjat is a powerful protection device commonly used by the Egyptians and usually drawn as the right eye, which represented the Sun. The left eye could also be used and that represented the Moon. They were also thought to represent the North and South halves of the Sun only. If both Udjats were drawn, that was a doubly powerful protection symbol. The basic use of an Udjat was to reflect the negativity aimed at it, so it was painted on houses, worn on jewellery, etc. and any negativity was reflected back to the sender. The word Udjat loosely means to be happy and safe, so the Amulet is a protection device that keeps the owner happy and safe!

☆ Amulet of Life (Ankh) ☆

The drawing of the Ankh represented life and was again very commonly used by the ancient Egyptians. Wearing the amulet protected and enriched your life and ensured a long and healthy one.

General Protection Devices

* Prayer
* White candles
* A Cross on your person or in your home
* A Crucifix
* Amulet/talisman in your pocket
* Garlic
* Horseshoe over your front door
* Spells
* A mobile phone
* Crystals
* Holy water sprinkled throughout your home
* Bunches of hazel twigs

* A corn dolly
* Incense and burning oils
* A large dog
* A crescent shaped pool of water outside your front door
* Wind chimes
* A Dream Catcher above your bed
* Red ribbons tied to any beams in your house
* Throwing a glass of water outside your front door before going out
* A Bible in your home

General Omens and their Mystical Meanings

* Four-leaf clover – general good luck
* Black cat crossing the road in front of you – general good luck (although in some countries, such as Bulgaria, this is general bad luck!)
* White heather – general good luck
* Finding a horseshoe – symbol of Epona Horse Goddess, good luck
* A ladybird near you – general good luck
* Wearing an item of clothing inside out – general good luck
* A wishbone – general good luck
* Breaking a drinking glass – general good luck
* Two magpies – general good luck
* Spiders – general good luck
* Crossing beneath a ladder – general bad luck
* Breaking a looking glass – general bad luck
* Spilling salt – general bad luck
* Opening an umbrella indoors – general bad luck

* Wearing a hat in bed – general bad luck
* Putting new shoes on a table – general bad luck
* Hearing an owl in the daytime – general bad luck
* Removing your wedding ring – general bad luck
* Wearing an opal – general good luck
* Keeping decorations up after Twelfth Night – general bad luck
* Red sky in the morning – bad weather
* Cows lying down – rain
* Something falling down your chimney – a storm brewing
* A cat washing its whiskers – a visitor coming

* A grey cat following you – a present or letter coming your way

* A spider spinning a web in the evening – someone is against you
* Dropping a knife – a lover will visit
* Itching feet – right: a successful journey; left: an unsuccessful journey
* Itching hands – right: money coming in; left: money going out
* Candle flame suddenly going out – a warning of bad fortune

General Dreams and their Mystical Meanings

* Flying or going upwards at a fast rate – success
* Falling or going downwards at a fast rate – failure
* Tunnels, tubes or trains – worries and changes
* Bright light – spiritual protection and success
* Gold and jewels – poverty
* Quarrelling – love

* Marriage – bad news, disappointment in love, difficulties
* Still water – financial success and happiness
* Moving water – business success
* Murky water – problems and mistakes
* Washing yourself – many lovers
* Broken teeth – bad luck

* Riding a bike – help is coming for a problem you have
* A party – happy times are coming
* A funeral – a change in your working life
* A boat – if you are sailing in it on calm waters your life will be happy, if you are fighting with rough waters, expect difficulties ahead
* Giant – successful outcome of a problem you've been experiencing
* A church – good fortune
* Feeling cold – good luck in a business venture

General Colours and their Mystical Meanings

* RED – Fire, energy, enthusiasm, attraction, loud, strong, attention seeking

* BLUE – Air, Water, calm, peace, clear, cool, individual, self-absorption

* GREEN – Water, Nature, healing, spiritual, cleansing, gentle, re-defining

* YELLOW – sunshine, happiness, newness, belief, optimistic, forward moving

* PURPLE – night, attraction, sensuous, giving, generous, flowering, originality

* ORANGE – stone, thirsty, hungry, liquid, moving, growing, excitement, pleasure

* BROWN – Earth, wise, patient, strong, solid, reliable, dependable, energy conductor

* WHITE – spirit, clouds, moon, quiet, silent, soft, meditation, pure, true, enclosing

* BLACK – space, empty, square, rigid, defined, mystical, thick, other worldly

* GOLD – worldly success, glitter, attraction
* BRONZE – mental success, gleam, meditation
* SILVER – spiritual success, shine, defining
* COPPER – health success, glow, giving

General Titles and their Mystical Meaning

GOD – Male Deity, Supreme Being, worshipped as having power over nature and human fortunes, Creator and ruler of Universe. Yang, Jesus, Ra, Sun, Father, Cernunnos, Air and Fire – Gold

GODDESS – Female Deity, Supreme Being, worshipped as having power over nature and human fortunes, Creator and ruler of Universe. Yin, Mary, Isis, Moon, Mother, Cerridwen, Earth and Water – Silver

ANGEL ELEMENTS – Divine messenger, spirit

Michael – Angel of Fire – Red

Gabriel – Angel of Water – Blue

Auriel – Angel of Earth – Green

Raphael – Angel of Air – White

SPIRITS – The element regarded as separable and animating the body. Too many to number, but every living thing has a spirit including all plants and animals

WITCH – Woman, Sorceress,

attuned to the use of magic. Passive, warm, female, adapting, blood, night, cauldron, birth, Cancer, Aquarius and Leo

MAGICIAN – Male Witch attuned to the use of magic. Positive, strong, united, metal, dragon, time, afternoon, Libra, Scorpio and Virgo

SORCERER – Man or Woman practising Witchcraft, heat, intelligence, attachment, withering, brightness, noon, Taurus and Gemini

ADEPT – Occult Sage, flexible, movement, love, wealth, male, understanding, mid-day, Aries and Taurus

SOOTH-SAYER – Diviner, growth, male, power, release, tears, horse, morning, divination, Aquarius and Pisces

HEALER – Restorer of health, emotional, moving, endurance, female, concentration, midnight, Scorpio, Sagittarius and Virgo

SCRYER – Diviner, quiet, rest, sleep, female, waiting, silence, protection, snow, dawn, Capricorn, Aquarius and Virgo

MONDAY – Moon

TUESDAY – Mars

WEDNESDAY – Mercury

THURSDAY – Jupiter

FRIDAY – Venus

SATURDAY – Saturn

SUNDAY – Sun

Karryaltar

In these stressful and hurried times it is immensely important for each individual to spare a few moments for meditation, worship or prayer which are all healing mechanisms for the self. A Karryaltar allows you to take this time-out whenever and wherever it suits you. Witches particularly are keen to worship outdoors due to the vibrant contact with nature, however everyone, no matter what their belief, can now have a portable Altar (even to take to work). You can create your own small altar which will be of no hindrance, but when unpacked can create a huge link between the psyche and the spiritual.

The idea behind the Karryaltar is simply a small, cardboard case with a foam insert which contains everything you need in miniature for a portable altar devoted to Wiccan worship. It can obviously be modified to suit Christianity, Jewish and any other religious worship. For these purposes the Karryaltar is explained for Wiccan worship.

The Karryaltar should be

different colours for different strengths: green would be mostly concerned with healing; blue would be mostly concerned with communicating; gold would be mostly concerned with finances; pink would be mostly concerned with love; or you could have a general Karryaltar which would probably be black and contain all the colours you would need in the forms of candles, ribbons, crystals, etc. This could then be carried around easily whatever your purpose!

To use simply lay the altar cloth over the case and arrange the contents neatly on top to display your altar. Now you can be free to travel and worship at any time and in any place!

☆ Usage ☆

Take it with you to festivals, travelling, parties, sole or group meditation and worship in the countryside, healing visits, on holiday or staying with friends.

☆ Contents ☆

Rolled up altar cloth, two white candles, chalice, one coloured candle, a bunch of silk flowers, pebble, incense holder and sticks, and this book, which contains instructions on Green Magic, incorporating spells, pictures of the Goddess and all you need to know about getting started.

☆ Ephemeris ☆

A very useful book listing tables of astrological data with which you can then find out your magical feast days, personal days, and so on.

☆ Finally ☆

Whilst compiling this book I had various messages and visits from the Ether encouraging me, and although I have tried to write in a humorous way, it is an honest and truthful attempt to explain the basic mysteries of Witchcraft and how to learn them for yourself. I truly believe that the Goddess inspired me to write this book as an easy guide for all those interested in following the Green Way of Witchcraft, and I hope it touches you and starts you on your journey. May your Spirit and the Goddess bless you all.

GILLY SERGIEV

(Henut Tawi)